MORALITY AND BEYOND

MORALITY
AND
BEYOND

PAUL TILLICH

Foreword by
William Schweiker

Westminster John Knox Press
Louisville, Kentucky

This book was originally published in 1963 by Harper & Row, Publishers, in the Religious Perspective Series edited by Ruth Nanda Anshen. First Harper Torchbook edition published in 1966.

First Westminster John Knox Press edition published in 1995 by arrangement with HarperSanFrancisco, a division of HarperCollins Publishers, Inc.

Published by Westminster John Knox Press
Louisville, Kentucky

Grateful acknowledgment is made to The University of Chicago Press to reprint chapters 4 and 5 of this book from *The Protestant Era* by Paul Tillich, published in 1948 and copyright 1948 by the University of Chicago. Chapter 4, "The Transmoral Conscience," originally appeared in *Crozer Quarterly*, Vol. XXII (1945), no. 4; chapter 5, "Ethics in a Changing World," originally appeared in *Religion and the Modern World* (Philadelphia: University of Pennsylvania Press, 1941).

This book is printed on acid-free paper that meets the American National Standards Institute Z39.48 standard. ∞

PRINTED IN THE UNITED STATES OF AMERICA

99 00 01 02 03 04 — 10 9 8 7 6 5 4 3

Library of Congress Cataloging-in-Publication Data

Tillich, Paul, 1886-1965.
    Morality and beyond / Paul Tillich ; foreword by William
Schweiker. — 1st Westminster John Knox Press ed.
        p.   cm. — (Library of theological ethics)
    Originally published : 1st ed. New York : Harper & Row, © 1963, in
series: Religious perspectives ; v. 9.
      ISBN 0-664-25564-7 (alk. paper)
    1. Christian ethics. 2. Religion and ethics. I. Title
II. Series.
    BJ251.T47   1995
    241—dc20   94-38997

Contents

General Editors' Introduction

The field of theological ethics possesses in its literature an abundant inheritance concerning religious convictions and the moral life, critical issues, methods, and moral problems. The Library of Theological Ethics is designed to present a selection of important texts that would otherwise be unavailable for scholarly purposes and classroom use. The series will engage the question of what it means to think theologically and ethically. It is offered in the conviction that sustained dialogue with our predecessors serves the interests of responsible contemporary reflection. Our more immediate aim in offering it, however, is to enable scholars and teachers to make more extensive use of classic texts as they train new generations of theologians, ethicists, and ministers.

The volumes included in the Library will comprise a variety of types. Some will make available English-language texts and translations that have fallen out of print; others will present new translations of texts previously unavailable in English. Still others will offer anthologies or collections of significant statements about problems and themes of special importance. We hope that each volume will encourage contemporary theological ethicists to remain in conversation with the rich and diverse heritage of their discipline.

ROBIN W. LOVIN
DOUGLAS F. OTTATI
WILLIAM SCHWEIKER

Foreword

William Schweiker

Paul Tillich, one of the great Protestant theologians of the twentieth century, addresses in *Morality and Beyond* a basic problem in moral theory: the relation between morality and the religious. Tillich insists that morality is essentially religious and that theological ethics must be seen as present in each part of systematic theology. In this respect, Tillich's moral vision is as challenging and timely as it was when first written.[1] Too often Christian ethicists and moral philosophers ignore the demands of theological reflection; contemporary theologians are given to moral exhortation in place of careful ethical reflection. Yet the question of the relation between morality and religion continues to fuel public debate, especially in an increasingly interdependent world of diverse and competing moral, cultural, and religious outlooks. A reconsideration of this present volume in the Library of Theological Ethics should prove helpful.

Morality and Beyond was initially published in 1963. The first three chapters were originally given as the Jacob Ziskind Memorial Lectures at Dartmouth College. The last two chapters are taken from Tillich's *The Protestant Era*, published by the University of Chicago Press, 1948. Thus the volume represents Tillich's mature moral thought. It is not surprising, then, that Tillich dedicated this book to his colleague and friend Reinhold Niebuhr of Union Theological Seminary, who was the most prominent Christian social

1

ethicist at that time. In this foreword, I want to explore the context and features of Tillich's argument, concluding with remarks about the significance of this text for current work in ethics.

TILLICH AND MODERN ETHICS

Paul Tillich states the basic challenge facing ethics as "Can we point to something that transcends both graceless moralism and normless relativism in ethical theory and action?"[2] Tillich was certain that what turns people from Christian morality to secular ethics is the loss of the reality of *grace*, the power to accept the unacceptable person, and the turn to moralistic preaching centered on religious and moral law. Yet he was equally certain that unless principles for right action are rooted in being and thus in some religious depth to existence, they could never escape relativism. The purpose of this book is to show that the reality of grace is the principle of morality rooted in being itself.

This concern with moralism and relativism in terms of a genuinely theological ethics locates Tillich's argument within the context of dominant impulses in modern ethics. First, modern moral philosophers have insisted that morality is autonomous, unrelated to religion.[3] The question of what is right and good must be determined on grounds other than appeal to God and God's will because one can always ask whether obedience to the divine will is itself good. Yet to ask that question is to demand a standard outside of the will of God. Ethics is thus autonomous, independent of religion.

Second, in reaction to nineteenth- and early twentieth-century liberal theologians, from Friedrich Schleiermacher to Albrecht Ritschl, Wilhelm Herrmann, and the Social Gospelers, who often granted the autonomy of morals, many twentieth-century theologians have attempted to reassert the distinctiveness of Christian ethics. This was done, as in the case of Karl Barth, through the revealed Word and command of God or, more recently, by appeal to the distinct practices, beliefs, and narratives of the Christian community insofar as these constitute a distinctive way of life. In making these arguments, theologians claim that the validity of Christian ethics can be established only internal to Christian beliefs or God's commands. Once again, the connection between religion and general moral reflection seems cut.

Tillich rejected both these options throughout his theological career. He consistently opposed the idea that philosophical thinking could be severed from its religious depths, from *ecstatic reason* as he called it. Tillich also consistently opposed forms of theological reflection, seen in the work of Barth and others, that seemed to center solely on dogmatic propositions and biblical discourse. Behind each of these positions Tillich believed one would find graceless moralism, ethical relativism, and the reduction of reason to merely technical rationality. *Morality and Beyond,* along with his other theological, political, and ethical writings, attempts to counter these impulses in modern thought.

For Tillich, the moral aim is "becoming a person within a community of persons." The task of this book is to show that this aim is essentially religious. Insofar as this can be shown, then the modern philosophical attempt to sever the connection between religion and morality is foiled at the outset. But by the same token, the demand that this places upon the theologian is not to establish the particularity of the Christian moral vision, but rather to show how Christian faith answers the moral aim. Tillich's ethics seeks to avoid moralism and relativism, and in terms of conceptual structure, to relate properly ethical thinking to systematic theology. The attempt to do so places Tillich's ethical thought at odds with dominant impulses in modern ethics and twentieth-century theology.

TILLICH'S THEONOMOUS ETHICS

Christian theologians earlier in this century were troubled by the claim made famous by Immanuel Kant that theological ethics was necessarily *heteronomous* because the person is bound by a

foreign will, the will of God. If this is the case, then moral norms
are relative to the will of God and have no grounding in reality;
the defining feature of morality is unquestioned obedience. In
order to counter this challenge, Paul Tillich and others introduced
the idea of *theonomy* into a Christian version of morality. For
Tillich, this concept was also to provide the means to avoid moralism and relativism. He argued that the moral law is simply the law
of our essential nature. It is, then, neither something we impose
on ourselves (autonomy) nor something imposed on us by a foreign will or power (heteronomy). The Christian message is that
true freedom is theonomous; the moral law of God is nothing else
than our true being. What does this mean?

Tillich's ethics revolves around three arguments needed to
counter moralism and relativism. First, he argues that the moral
act aims at actualization of self; that is, at constituting the person
as a centered self. "For the ethical problem this means," Tillich
writes, "that the moral act is always a victory over disintegrating
forces and that its aim is the actualization of man as a centered
and therefore free person."[4] The experience of the imperative to
actualize the self is found in conscience, "the silent voice," as
Tillich puts it, of our essential nature judging our actual lives.
The moral law is nothing else than our essential nature formulated in terms of an imperative. To act on this law is to act out of
freedom, since it is to act according to our essential being.

Second, Tillich shows that this law is not a matter of psychology or social custom, but is the will of God. That is, Tillich seeks
to demonstrate the religious source of morality. He writes:

The "Will of God" for us is precisely our essential being with all of
its potentialities, our created nature declared as "very good" by
God, as, in terms of the Creation myth, He "saw everything that
he made." For us the "Will of God" is manifest in our essential
being; and only because of this can we accept the moral imperative
as valid. It is not a strange law that demands our obedience, but the
"silent voice" of our own nature as man, and as man with an individual character.[5]

Tillich argues, then, that the moral law articulates what we most essentially are—centered persons in relation to God as the ground and power of being—as an imperative for how to live amid the ambiguities of actual life. The will of God is nothing else than the good of essential being. This means, as Tillich puts it, that "morality does not depend on any concrete religion; it is religious in its very essence."[6]

Tillich then seeks to establish morality in a way to avoid any simple relativism or a heteronomous conception of moral demands. The fact is, however, that our actual being is not our true being. Our lives are marked by fragmentation. "The voice of man's essential being is silenced, step by step; and his disintegrating self, his depersonalization, shows the nature of the anti-moral act and, by contrast, the nature of the moral act."[7] Because of our estrangement from our essential being, we encounter the moral law as an imperative for action. This estrangement is heard in the testimony of conscience against the self. Graceless moralism is born of the fact that fallen creatures hear the demand to actualize their essential nature in conscience as a heteronomous law demanding obedience. How then is this ethical problem—the conflict between self-integration and disintegration—to be answered beyond moralism?

For Tillich, the answer is found in love, *agape*, as the ultimate principle of morality. This is the third argument in his ethics. *Agape*, Tillich insists, "points to the transcendent source of the content of the moral imperative" and unifies our actual nature with our essential being.[8] *Agape* overcomes the estrangement of fallen existence from the goodness of created, essential being. This love, *agape*, also draws within itself justice, as the acknowledgment of the other person as a person, and the power to act. In this way, *agape* is an answer to graceless moralism, while at the same time an *agapistic* ethics avoids the peril of moral relativism.

Tillich's ethics stresses the demand for the actualization of life against disintegrating forces. He conceives of this in terms of the reunification in *agape* of actual life with essential being. By acting on the moral law in obedience to our essential nature, a higher mode of being is actualized, that is, the person as a centered self. In this way, the essential connection between morality and religion is asserted so that moralism and relativism are avoided.

THE CHALLENGE OF TILLICH
TO THEOLOGICAL ETHICS

The significance of Paul Tillich's contribution to twentieth-century Christian theology is beyond question. His contribution to theological ethics is more difficult to assess. The reason for this is in part the fact that Tillich rejected the idea of a separate discipline called theological ethics. As he states in the opening pages of *Morality and Beyond*, theological ethics is treated separately only as a matter of expedience. But the other reason that Tillich's contribution to theological ethics is difficult to assess is that during his career, he reconceived theological ethics as the theology of culture.[9] Even the text of *Morality and Beyond* can be seen as an astute theological analysis of modern culture caught between the forces of moralism and modern ethical relativism. Granting the ambiguity in Tillich's thought about the actual status of theological ethics as a discipline, we can still isolate features of his work that pose challenges to current theological ethics.

For Tillich, morality is grounded in our essential being. In this respect, his ethics stands in continuity with traditional Roman Catholic natural law ethics and other forms of moral realism. What is morally right and good is the realization through action of human natural potentialities. The difference, as James M. Gustafson has noted, is that natural law ethics is casuistic because moral reason is directed to determining the rightness or wrongness of specific acts.[10] Tillich's ethics, in contrast, verges on intuitionism because of its appeal to the "silent voice" of conscience about essential nature. Despite similar beginning points, natural law ethics and Tillich's ethics reach divergent practical conclusions.

The challenge Tillich's work poses to theological ethics on this point is how to specify the precise relation between casuistry, that is, reasoning about moral cases, and claims about human nature. If we are going to reason rightly about moral cases, must we assume something about the nature of human beings? If we cannot reach agreement about the nature of human life or its good—a consensus difficult to reach in wildly pluralistic societies—does this invalidate casuistic thinking? Theologians and philosophers currently have attempted to sever the connection between casuistry and claims about human nature.[11] Tillich's ethics, while itself deficient on matters of casuistry, challenges this move by questioning the point of morality itself. If morality is about the realization of human potentialities, then some conception of human nature seems required in addressing practical moral questions. The demand on the casuist is either to show that this is not the point of morality so that no claim about human nature is needed in ethics or, conversely, to provide a different account of human nature, such as that found in traditional natural law ethics.

This leads to another challenge of Tillich's thought to current theological ethics. For Tillich, morality is grounded in our essential being. But what that means, according to him, is that morality finds its source in God as the ground and power of being. Ethics is in this respect necessarily theological in character. This raises two questions. First, how is the idea of God related to some conception of what is morally good? That is, even if one grants Tillich's claim about the religious character of morality, it is another question to ask about the *content* of claims about God and goodness. How does a conception of the good, whether grounded in claims about human nature or historically specific beliefs, relate to Christian ideas about God and *agape*?[12] Some moral theorists argue that in ethics we need only a thin theory of the good, because the point of the moral life in a pluralistic society is just relations between persons rather than establishing the human good. At issue then are the substance of claims about the human good, the status of those claims, their place in ethics, and the relation between those claims and discourse about God. This leads to the second question: Given the fact of moral diversity on this planet, can one sustain the claim that morality is theistic? Indeed, is that claim actually needed in ethics? Is an appeal to *agape* morally adequate in our time? Put differently, Tillich's concern to combat moralism and relativism must be rethought in terms of the reality of moral pluralism and also of debates about how to understand moral goodness.

The final challenge Tillich's thought poses to theological ethics is at the level of basic moral problems. For Tillich, the moral problem is the fragmentation of life; the moral act is a victory of self-integration against forces that lead to human estrangement. This means that the power to act is essential to how Tillich conceives of the human good because only through the exercise of power in action is life realized. Now in our time, technology has radically increased human power to the point that we can alter the environment and even the human species. This makes the reality of power and human responsibility basic to contemporary ethical reflection.[13] Tillich addresses these matters in terms of the dominance of technical rationality in the modern world and also theologically by understanding the term *God* as symbolizing the power of being itself. The question that remains open, however, is the extent to which claims about rationality and the symbol *God* can contribute to current ethical reflection on the reality of human power and the demands of responsibility.

Thus Tillich challenges theological ethics in terms of patterns of practical moral reasoning, the relation between claims about God and those of moral goodness, and also the contribution of theological discourse to reflection on human power and responsibility. Any assessment of his ethics in terms of the history of thought or contemporary ethical reflection must engage his work on each of these points.

CONCLUSION

Morality and Beyond is a slender volume. And yet, remarkably, in these few pages Tillich addresses basic theoretical questions in theological ethics. It is for this reason that his work warrants careful consideration by theologians, philosophers, and students of ethics. The publication of *Morality and Beyond* in the Library of Theological Ethics should make an engagement with Tillich's thought all the more possible.

NOTES

1. For a fuller discussion of these matters, see William Schweiker, *Responsibility and Christian Ethics* (Cambridge: Cambridge University Press, forthcoming); see also Dietz Lange, *Ethik in evangelischer Perspektive* (Göttingen: Vanderhoeck & Ruprecht, 1992).

2. Paul Tillich, *Morality and Beyond* (New York: Harper & Row, 1963), 14.

3. See Franklin I. Gamwell, *The Divine Good: Modern Moral Theory and the Necessity of God* (San Francisco: HarperCollins, 1990).

4. Ibid., 21.

5. Ibid., 24.

6. Ibid., 64.

7. Ibid., 21.

8. Ibid., 40.

9. For an attempt to rethink the theology of culture in terms of theological ethics, see William Schweiker, "Hermeneutics, Ethics, and the Theology of Culture: Concluding Reflections" in *Meanings in Texts and Actions: Questioning Paul Ricoeur,* ed. David E. Klemm and William Schweiker (Charlottesville, Va.: University Press of Virginia, 1993), 292–313.

10. James M. Gustafson, *Protestant and Roman Catholic Ethics: Prospects for Rapprochement* (Chicago: University of Chicago Press, 1978).

11. See, for example, Albert R. Jonsen and Stephen Toulmin, *The Abuse of Casuistry: A History of Moral Reasoning* (Berkeley: University of California Press, 1988).

12. See Iris Murdoch, *Metaphysics as a Guide to Morals* (New York: Penguin Press, Allen Lane, 1993).

13. See Hans Jonas, *The Imperative of Responsibility: In Search of an Ethic for the Technological Age*, trans. Hans Jonas and David Herr (Chicago: University of Chicago Press, 1984). Also see the essays by Karl-Otto Apel, Robin W. Lovin, Wolfgang Huber, and William Schweiker from the Conference on Realism and Responsibility in Contemporary Ethics published in *The Journal of Religion* 73, no. 4 (1993).

MORALITY AND BEYOND

Introduction

Theological ethics is an element of systematic theology, present in each of its parts. As a matter of expediency, it is often treated separately in lectures and studies because of the immensity of the material to be covered and the justified desire, on the scholar's part, to deal with particular problems comprehensively. The problem to be discussed in the following five chapters is the age-old question of how the moral is related to the religious.

It is urgent to raise this question again in view of the present character both of the church's preaching and of philosophical ethics. The latter either shares the general retreat of analytical philosophy into logical and semantic problems or continues the discussion of value theory (which in itself is a retreat from ontological inquiry), or else it undermines the possibility of ethical norms by pure pragmatism or pure existentialism, although this assumption of purity is a delusion.

More important, however, is the state of preaching and teaching in the church, both Catholic and Protestant, and most conspicuously in Protestantism. The gospel (*euangelion,* "good news"), the message of reconciliation and reunion with God as the Ground and Aim of our being has been transformed into a multiplicity of laws, partly doctrinal and partly ethical. The moral "yoke" that Jesus wished to make easy has only been made heavier, and the message of grace has largely been lost, despite the numerous liturgical prayers for the forgiveness of sins. They do not express the vision that appears in

Paul's Letters and John's Gospel, or is expressed in the seventh petition of the Lord's Prayer—"save us from the evil one"—namely, the image of a demonic power ruling the universe and driving man into separation from God and into hostility against Him. The prayers for forgiveness have, for many people, only the function of relieving the uneasy conscience produced by trespasses against traditional and often absurd rules of behavior, mostly of a prohibitive character. But they do not express the great paradox, that there is a reunion with the eternal "Ground of our being" without "right" action on our part, without our being "good people," or the "people of good will." Therefore, despite liturgical formulae, hymns, and the reading of lessons from the Pauline Epistles, the message of grace has been lost. Grace as the power of accepting the person who is unacceptable, and of healing the person who is mortally sick, has disappeared behind the preaching of the religious and moral law.

It is understandable that people, in view of this graceless moralism, turn to secular ethics. But when they find nothing more than the logical analysis of ethical theory, they turn easily to a cynical relativism or to a totalitarian absolutism in ethics, each often a consequence of the other. The question implicit in this situation is: Can we point to something that transcends both graceless moralism and normless relativism in ethical theory and moral action?

The response of Christianity is the message that a new reality has appeared with the coming of the Christ, a power of being in which we can participate, and out of which true thought and right action can follow, however fragmentarily. We find analogous affirmations in other religions and even in secular movements of an implicitly religious character, such as nationalism, socialism, and liberal humanism. Being precedes action in everything that is, including man, although in man as the bearer of freedom, previous action also determines present being. This answer stands in opposition to both moral legalism and amoral lawlessness. It affirms morality and points beyond it to its religious foundation.

"Religious principles of moral action" is the subject matter of the first three chapters of this volume, which form a kind of unity, and were originally delivered under the same title as the Jacob Ziskind Memorial Lectures at Dartmouth College. The last two chapters, taken from my book *The Protestant Era,* discuss decisive consequences of the basic analysis—Chapter IV demonstrating the liberation of the moral conscience by its transmoral foundation, and Chapter V the possibility of conquering ethical relativism through the united principles of *agape* ("love") and *kairos* ("the right moment"). I am grateful to the University of Chicago Press for granting me permission to reprint these two chapters.

The manner in which this book has come into existence accounts for some repetition and for occasional incompleteness. Despite these limitations, it is my hope that the study will help to remove the obsolete conflict between reason-determined ethics and faith-determined ethics. It attempts to do so by showing that the religious principles dwell within the principles of moral action. If morality is intrinsically religious, as religion is intrinsically ethical, neither is dependent on the other, and neither can be substituted for the other.

I am deeply grateful to Mrs. Elizabeth Wood who has again improved my English style as she did for the three volumes of my sermons.

This book is dedicated to Reinhold Niebuhr, after thirty years of friendship and dialogue. The tension between the ethical, which he has represented, and the ontological, for which I have stood, has proved to be an important door by which to enter into the mysteries of theology and life.

Not forgotten is the decisive role he played in bringing my family and myself to the United States shortly after the Nazis came to power and forced me to leave Germany in 1933. Ever since, we have worked together in mutual support, criticism, and *agape*.

PAUL TILLICH

East Hampton, Long Island
July 1963

I

The Religious Dimension
of the Moral Imperative

In the first three chapters of this book, the immanence of the religious in the moral shall be considered from three directions. The first chapter deals with the religious *dimension* of the moral imperative, the second with the religious *source* of the moral demands, and the third with the religious *element* in moral motivation.

To understand the meaning of the phrase "moral imperative," we must distinguish the three basic functions of the human spirit: morality, culture, and religion. When we call them functions of man's "spirit," we point to the dynamic unity of body and mind, of vitality and rationality, of the conscious and the unconscious, of the emotional and the intellectual. In every function of the human spirit the whole person is involved, and not merely one part or one element. As I have often insisted, we must revive the term "spirit" as designating a natural quality of man. It cannot be replaced by "mind" because "mind" is overweighted by its intellectual aspect.

None of the three functions of the spirit ever appears in isolation from the other two. They must be distinguished, nonetheless, because they are able to relate to each other in many different ways. Most concisely, we might say: morality is the constitution of the bearer of the spirit, the centered person;

culture points to the creativity of the spirit and also to the totality of its creations; and religion is the self-transcendence of the spirit toward what is ultimate and unconditioned in being and meaning.

The first of these functions is our direct and primary subject. But in order to deal with it adequately we must continually refer to the other two. This presents a difficulty hardly to be resolved in an essay such as this, and only overcome within a system that comprises the whole of man's interpretation of himself and the meaning of his life (which I undertook to develop in my *Systematic Theology*). The present study must presuppose but cannot develop such an interpretation; however, we must refer to it, and derive from it a possible solution of the problem at hand—"the religious principles of moral action."

The moral act establishes man as a person, and as a bearer of the spirit. It is the unconditional character of the moral imperative that gives ultimate seriousness both to culture and to religion. Without it culture would deteriorate into an aesthetic or utilitarian enterprise, and religion into an emotional distortion of mysticism. It was the prophetic message, as recorded in the Old Testament, that contrasted the moral imperative, in terms of the demand for justice, with both the culture and the religion of its time. The message is one of ultimate seriousness and has no equivalent in any other religion. The seriousness of Christianity depends upon it, as does also any ultimate seriousness in Western culture. Science and the arts, politics, education—all become empty and self-destructive if, in their creation, the moral imperative is disregarded. The imperative exhibits itself in scientific and artistic honesty to the extent of self-sacrifice; in one's commitment to humanity and justice in social relations and political actions; and in the love of one toward the other, as a consequence of experiencing the divine love. These are examples which demonstrate that, without the immanence of the moral imperative, both culture and religion disintegrate because of lack of ultimate seriousness.

The moral imperative is the command to become what one potentially is, a *person* within a community of persons. Only man, in the limit of our experience, can become a person, because only man is a completely centered self, having himself as a self in the face of a world to which he belongs and from which he is, at the same time, separated. This dual relation to his world, belongingness and separation, makes it possible for him to ask questions and find answers, to receive and make demands. As a centered self and individual, man can respond in knowledge and action to the stimuli that reach him from the world to which he belongs; but because he also *confronts* his world, and in this sense is free from it, he can respond "responsibly," namely, after deliberation and decision rather than through a determined compulsion. This is his greatness, but also his danger: it enables him to act *against* the moral demand. He can surrender to the disintegrating forces which tend to control the personal center and to destroy its unity. But before we pursue this line of thought, we must consider more thoroughly some of our concepts up to this point.

Man has a world, namely, a structured whole of innumerable parts, a *cosmos,* as the Greeks called it, because of its structured character which makes it accessible to man through acts of creative receiving and transforming. Having a world is more than having environment. Of course, man, like any other being, has environment; but in contrast to the higher animals, for example, he is not bound to it. He can transcend it in any direction, in imagination, thought and action (e.g., social utopias or ontological concepts or space exploration). Man has "world" through every part of his environment. His encounter with any of the objects surrounding him is always an encounter with the universe manifest in a particular object. Man never encounters *this* tree only as *this* tree, but also as *tree,* one of many trees, as an example of the species tree (in itself a special manifestation of the universal power of being).

Such an encounter presupposes freedom from the particular, and the ability to see the universal within the particular. The manifestation of this freedom is language. Language lives in universals. It is one and the same thing to have world, to transcend environment, and to speak in concepts and meaningful propositions. All this constitutes man's essential freedom and is the presupposition of man's experience of the moral imperative.

The moral imperative is the demand to become actually what one is essentially and therefore potentially. It is the power of man's being, given to him by nature, which he shall actualize in time and space. His true being shall become his actual being—this is the moral imperative. And since his true being is the being of a person in a community of persons, the moral imperative has this content: to become a person. Every moral act is an act in which an individual self establishes itself as a person.

Therefore, a moral act is not an act in obedience to an external law, human or divine. It is the inner law of our true being, of our essential or created nature, which demands that we actualize what follows from it. And an antimoral act is not the transgression of one or several precisely circumscribed commands, but an act that contradicts the self-realization of the person as a person and drives toward disintegration. It disrupts the centeredness of the person by giving predominance to partial trends, passions, desires, fears, and anxieties. The central control is weakened, often almost removed. And when this happens, and other partial trends also aspire to predominance, the self is split, and the conflicting trends make it their battlefield. The "will," in the sense of a self that acts from the centered totality of its being, is enslaved. Freedom is replaced by compulsion. Deliberation and decision, the hallmarks of freedom, become mere façades for overwhelming drives that predetermine the decision. The voice of man's essential being is silenced, step by step; and his disintegrating self, his depersonalization, shows the nature of the antimoral act and, by contrast, the nature of the moral act.

The moral act as the self-actualization of the centered self or the constitution of the person as a person, has analogies in the realm of all living beings, including man from the biological point of view. The analogy to the diminution or loss of centeredness in man is the psychosomatic phenomenon of disease. In disease, some processes that are necessary elements in the whole of a life process take an independent course and endanger the functioning of the whole. The cancerous growth of parts of the body is the most illuminating analogy to what happens in the centered self when particular trends conquer the center and destroy the unity of balanced trends. The analogy between the antimoral act and bodily disease is in many (somehow in all) cases more than an analogy. Both are expressions of the universal ambiguity of life, according to which the processes of self-integration are continuously combated by movements toward disintegration. For the ethical problem this means that the moral act is always a victory over disintegrating forces and that its aim is the actualization of man as a centered and therefore free person.

At this point a short semantic remark seems necessary. In this study, I use the terms "morality," "morals," and "moral" throughout most of the text. And sometimes the term "ethical" appears. There would be no confusion if, as I now suggest, we defined ethics as the "science of the moral." But this is not a generally accepted definition, the chief reason being that the word "moral," through historical accidents, has received several distorting connotations. Since the eighteenth century, at least in Europe, it has carried the implication of "moralism" in the sense of graceless legalistic ethics. And in the United States, it has, under the influence of Puritanism, taken on a sexual signification: to be "amoral" means to be sexually lawless, or at least to deny conventional sex ethics. Because of these two connotations, one has tried to replace "moral" by "ethical." Were this generally accepted, however, the term "ethical" would soon acquire the connotation of "moral," and there would be no change. Therefore, I recommend that "ethical" be reserved for the *theory* of morals, and that the term "moral" and its derivatives be purged of those associations, and used to describe the moral act itself in its fundamental significance.

We have discussed the nature of the moral act, its all-permeating character, and its immanence in the other two chief functions of man's spirit—the cultural and the religious. We must now ask: what is the religious dimension of the moral imperative, and (in Chapter II) what is the relation of cultural creativity to morality?

In answer to the first question, we can say: the religious dimension of the moral imperative is its unconditional character. This, of course, leads to a subsequent question: why is the moral imperative unconditional, and in which respects can one call it so, and in which not? In our daily life we use innumerable imperatives; but most of them are conditional: "you ought to leave *now*, if you wish to catch your plane." But perhaps you prefer to stay, even though you miss the plane. This obviously is a conditional imperative. However, if getting to the plane should be a matter of life and death, as, for example, in the case of a physician who must immediately operate upon a patient, the conditional imperative becomes unconditional. To miss the plane through negligence would then be an antimoral act, and would affect the person of the physician in a disintegrating manner. We might compare the disintegrating effect that the failure to save a drowning woman has on the main character in Camus' *The Fall*.

There are many cases in which conditional imperatives have some bearing on an unconditional imperative. The missing of the plane might also arouse anxiety in those who expect the arrival of a friend. And there are cases in which several imperatives compete for supreme validity, and in which the decision is a moral risk. But despite these "mixed" cases, the moral imperative in itself is, as Immanuel Kant called it, "categorical" rather than "hypothetical," or as I would say, unconditional as opposed to conditional.

We may ask, however, whether a moral decision can stand under an unconditional imperative if the decision is a moral risk—the "risk" implying that it might prove to be the wrong decision. The answer to this question is that the unconditional character does not refer to the content, but to the form of the moral decision. Whichever side of a moral alternative might be chosen, however great the risk in a bold decision may be, if it be a *moral* decision it is dependent only on the pure "ought to be" of the moral imperative. And should anyone be in doubt as to which of several possible acts conforms to the moral imperative, he should be reminded that each of them might be justified in a particular situation, but that whatever he chooses must be done with the consciousness of standing under an unconditional imperative. The doubt concerning the justice of a moral act does not contradict the certainty of its ultimate seriousness.

The assertion of the intrinsically religious character of the moral imperative can be criticized from different points of view. Theology can strongly affirm the unconditioned character of the moral imperative, but deny that this character makes it religious. Moral commands, one argues then, are religious because they are divine commandments. They are ultimately serious because they express the "Will of God."

This alone makes them unconditional. God could have willed differently, and we must open our eyes to His revelation in order to know what His Will actually is. Such an argument, of course, would exclude any kind of secular ethics. Not only the content but also the unconditional character of the moral imperative would have to be sanctioned by a divine command, and conserved in holy traditions or sacred books.

I maintain, however, that the term "Will of God" can and must be understood differently. It is not an external will imposed upon us, an arbitrary law laid down by a heavenly tyrant, who is strange to our essential nature and therefore whom we resist justifiably from the point of view of our nature. The "Will of God" for us is precisely our essential being with all its potentialities, our created nature declared as "very good" by God, as, in terms of the Creation myth, He "saw everything that he made." For us the "Will of God" is manifest in our essential being; and only because of this can we accept the moral imperative as valid. It is not a strange law that demands our obedience, but the "silent voice" of our own nature as man, and as man with an individual character.

But we must go one further step. We can say: to fulfill one's own nature is certainly a moral demand intrinsic in one's being. But why is it an unconditional imperative? Do I not have the right to leave my potentialities unfulfilled, to remain less than a person, to contradict my essential goodness, and thus to destroy myself? As a being that has the freedom of self-contradiction, I should have the right to this possibility, and to waste myself! The moral imperative is unconditional only if I choose to affirm my own essential nature, and *this is* a condition! The answer to this argument is the experience that has been expressed in the doctrine of the infinite value of every human soul in the view of the Eternal. It is not an external prohibition against self-destruction—bodily, psychologically, or morally—that we experience in states of despair, but the silent voice of our own being which denies us the right to self-destruction. It is the awareness of our belonging to a dimension that transcends our own finite freedom and our ability to affirm or to negate ourselves. So I maintain my basic assertion that the unconditional character of the moral imperative is its religious quality. No religious heteronomy, subjection to external commands, is implied if we maintain the immanence of religion in the moral command.

The intrinsically religious character of the moral imperative is indirectly denied by the philosophy of values. Its representatives think in terms of a hierarchy of values, in which the value of the holy may or may not find a place; when it does, it is often on the top of this pyramid, above the moral, legal, social, political, and economic values. For our problem, this means first of all that values lie above and below each other and that there can be no immanence of one within another. The value of the holy, for example. cannot be immanent in the value of the good, and conversely. The relationship is external and may lead to the elimination of one or the other —most frequently, in this case, the value of the holy.

A second character of the value theory has a considerable bearing on our problem. The establishment of values and their relationships presupposes a valuating subject, and the question arises: how can values that are relative to a valuating individual or group (e.g., pleasure values) be separated from values that are valid by their very nature regardless of personal or social attitudes? If there are such "absolute values" (absolute in the sense of being independent of a valuating subject), what is the source of their absoluteness, how can they be discovered, how are they related to reality, and what is their ontological standing? These questions lead unavoidably to a situation that the value theory by its very nature tries to avoid—namely, a doctrine of being, an ontology. For values have reality only if they are rooted in reality. Their validity is an expression of their ontological foundation. *Being pre-cedes value,* but value fulfills being. Therefore, the value theory, in its search for absolute values, is thrown back upon the ontological question of the source of values in being.

A third way in which the religious dimension of the moral imperative is questioned can be described as the attempt, with the help of psychological and sociological explanations, to deny the unconditional character of the moral altogether. The psychological impact of realities like the demanding and threatening parents, or of doctrines like that of the command-ing and punishing God, evokes the feeling of something un-conditionally serious from which there is no escape and with which there can be no compromise.

The same argument can be strengthened by sociological considerations. For example, one can derive, like Nietzsche, the shaping of the conscience of the masses from centuries of pressure exercised by the ruling groups, who did not hesitate to employ all, even the most cruel, tools of suppression— military, legal, educational, psychological. From generation to generation this pressure produced an increasing internaliza-tion of commands, namely, the sense of standing under an inner unconditional command, an absolute moral impera-tive.

This type of argument seems convincing. But it is circular because it presupposes what it tries to prove—the identity of two qualitatively different structures. In the one case, persons and groups are bound by traditions, conventions, and authori-ties, subjection to which is demanded by the conscience, which may be weak or strong, compromising or insistent, healthy or compulsory, reasonable or fanatic. Psychological or sociologi-cal explanations of such states of mind are fully justified. Nothing that happens in the mind should be exempt from psy-chological or sociological exploration and explanation. But within this structure of causation, another is manifest—what we might call the "structure of meaning" or, to use a famous medieval term revived by modern phenomenology, the structure of "intentionality" or the *noetic* structure (from *nous*, "mind"). This structure would be evident, for example, should a mathematician, psychologically and sociologically conditioned like everyone else, discover a new mathematical proposition. The validity of this proposition is independent of the series of conditions which made the discovery possible. In a similar way, the meaning of the unconditional in being and in what ought-to-be appears within the psychological and sociological processes which make its appearance possible. But its validity is not dependent on the structure in which it appears. Psychological and sociological pressures may provide occasion for the appearance of such structures; but they cannot produce the meaning of the unconditional. However strong the pressures be, they are themselves conditioned, and it is possible to contradict them and to be liberated from them, as, for example, from the father-image or from the socially produced conscience. This is not possible with regard to the unconditional character of the moral imperative. One can, of course, discard every particular content for the sake of another, but one cannot discard the moral imperative itself without the self-destruction of one's essential nature and one's eternal relationship. For these reasons, the attempts to undercut the unconditional character of the moral imperative by psychological and sociological arguments must fail.

There is, however, a more fundamental question, raised and thoroughly discussed by the ancient ethical philosophers, namely, the question of the moral aim. We have called it "becoming a person within a community of persons," and we have indicated that the centered person is the bearer of the spirit, its creativity, and its self-transcendence. Insofar as it is the moral aim to constitute and preserve the person with these potentialities, we can say that the moral imperative demands the actualization of man's created potentiality. But now the question arises: is this an unconditional demand? The answer depends on the idea of man's intrinsic aim, of the *telos* for which he is created. If the aim implies something above finitude and transitoriness, the fulfillment of this aim is infinitely significant, or unconditional in its seriousness. When Plato said that the *telos* of man is "to become as much as possible similar to the God," such a *telos* gives unconditional character to the moral imperative. If, however, the *telos* is, as in the hedonistic school, the greatest possible amount of pleasure to be derived from life, no unconditional imperative is at work, but merely the very much conditioned advice to calculate well what amount of pain must be suffered in order to attain to the greatest possible amount of pleasure. Between these two extremes of the definition of man's inner *telos* are several definitions which set a finite aim according to the formulation, but in which something unconditional with respect to the moral imperative shines through. This is true of utilitarianism, in which the moral imperative demands work for "the greatest happiness of the greatest number." Here pleasure is replaced by "happiness," and above all, it is not the individual happiness, but that of the many, which is the aim. And the happiness of the many is not possible without self-restraint in the individual's search for happiness. Therefore, a demand appears that cannot be derived from the merely natural trends of the individual, a demand that implies the acceptance of the other person as a person, and an unconditional element besides, whether acknowledged or not.

The Epicureans deal with the problems of the *telos* and the moral imperative from another angle. They also use the term "happiness," but for them happiness consists in the life of the spirit in community with friends, and in the creative participation in the cognitive and aesthetic values of their culture. The relationship to friends as well as to cultural creativity demands unconditional subjection to the norms and structures of friendship, knowledge, and beauty.

Nearest to Plato's definition of the human *telos* is Aristotle's thought that man's highest aim is participation in the eternal divine self-intuition. This state can be fully reached only by entering the eternal life above finite life. This does not mean that the individual has immortality but that, within time, he can participate in eternity through the "theoretical" life, the life of intuition. Wherever this state of participation is reached, there is *eudaimonia*, fulfillment under the guidance of a "good daimon," a half-divine power. To reach this goal is an unconditional imperative. And since the practical virtues are the precondition for fulfillment through participation in the divine, they also have unconditional validity.

We have used the Greek word *eudaimonia* (badly translated as "happiness") in order to point out the moral aim as described in several ethical schools. *Eudaimonia* belongs to those words that have suffered a marked deterioration in meaning. Most responsible for this process were the Stoic and Christian polemics against Epicureanism, which often unjustly confused Epicureanism with hedonism. The word in itself means fulfillment with divine help, and consequent happiness. This happiness does not exclude pleasure, but the pleasure is not the aim, nor is happiness itself the aim. It is the companion of fulfillment, reached together with it. If we derogate this concept of *eudaimonia,* we must also derogate the Christian hope for eternal blessedness. For, even though the Calvinist names the glory of God as the aim of his life, he experiences blessedness in fulfilling this aim and serving the glory of God. The same, of course, is true of *theosis* ("becoming Godlike"), *fruitio Dei* ("enjoying the intuition of the divine life"), or working for and participating in the "Kingdom of God" described as the aim of the individual man, of mankind, and the universe.

Happiness or blessedness as the emotional awareness of fulfillment is not in conflict with the unconditional, and therefore religious, character of the moral imperative. A conflict exists only when the function of self-transcendence in man's spirit is denied, and man is seen as totally imprisoned in his finitude. But this diminution of man to a finite process has rather rarely occurred in the history of thought. Even highly secularized philosophers were conscious of the function of self-transcendence in man's spirit, and consequently of the dimension of the unconditional or the religious dimension.

There are two concepts in the preceding discussion that have been frequently used without having been thoroughly discussed. The one is "conscience," the channel through which the unconditional character of the moral imperative is experienced, and the other is the term "religious" (in the title and in many other parts of this chapter). The concept of conscience will be fully discussed in Chapter IV. Regarding the concept of religion (which I have developed in much of my work), I can restrict myself to the following summary: the fundamental concept of religion is the state of being grasped by an ultimate concern, by an infinite interest, by something one takes unconditionally seriously. It is in view of this concept that we have formulated the main proposition of this chapter, namely, that there is a religious dimension in the moral imperative itself. Derived from the fundamental concept of religion is the traditional concept that religion is a particular expression, in symbols of thought and action, of such ultimate concern within a social group as, for example, a church. If the moral imperative were derived from religion in the traditional sense of the word, secular ethics would have to sever any ties with religion, for it rejects direct dependence on any particular religion. If, however, the religious element is intrinsic to the moral imperative, no conflict is necessary.

II

The Religious Source
of the Moral Demands

The first chapter avoided any detailed statement concerning the content of the moral imperative. It restricted itself to a discussion of the unconditional character of morality, whatever the moral demand might be, and however determined by historical and personal conditions. Its unconditional character was considered as its religious quality.

Undoubtedly the question of the ethical content—the question of what one must do—has already and persistently arisen in the minds of many readers. This question was not left totally unanswered; but the answer—that we must become what we essentially are, *persons*—is so formal that it does not offer any concrete advice. Yet such advice is necessary for the life of man. So also are principles, which are at the same time abstract and concrete, so that support for moral decisions can be derived from them. Are there such principles of moral action? If so, how can they be related to the ever changing conditions of existence? Is not ethical relativism the only possible answer, even in view of the unconditional character of the moral imperative?

The first problem of this chapter is to consider the positive aspects and the limitations of ethical relativism. For relativism is the predominant ethical theory and, in many respects, also a widespread moral practice. The facts that support this theory are obvious. The pronounced difference between primitive and modern ethics and between Western and Eastern, feudal and bourgeois, liberal-humanist and neo-collectivist morality, and the difference in ethical attitudes to the same event in the same locality by diverse social strata, diverse religious groups, and diverse generations strongly support ethical relativism.

For a certain time anthropologists dealing with primitive cultures were the champions of ethical relativism. Ever since the eighteenth century, anthropological research has shown a particular interest in the ethics of primitive man. His morality was supposed to demonstrate the conditioning of our own ethical ideas, whether feudal or bourgeois, Christian or humanist. Particular laws pertaining, for example, to killing, stealing, lying, and so forth, in one culture were compared with corresponding but different (and sometimes contradicting) laws in another culture, and the conclusion was drawn that there is no common ground in ethical thought among separated cultures. Ethics, according to this view, is culturally conditioned, and therefore ethics of different cultures are as different as the cultures themselves. In both cultural anthropology and popular understanding, such concepts are still widespread despite the fact that a sharp reaction has arisen against the primitive character of this method. We have learned (partly through the insight that a living reality is a structural unity, a *Gestalt,* and not a mechanical composite) that cultures are wholes, and that we cannot compare parts of them with parts of others, but must understand the significance of the particulars in the light of the whole. Then we may discover that the contrast of ethical demands in separated cultures is not a contradiction, but a different expression of a common fundamental principle. Ignorance of this insight has produced much naïve relativism in popular thought and unfortunately also among scholars when they unintentionally become philosophers. The method of structural analysis is a warning against a primitive use of the "primitives" in the argument for ethical relativism.

A positive and constructive criticism of the relativistic theories is embodied in the doctrine of the natural moral law. It is a very old, famous, and still rather vital theory that man by nature (in Christianity by creation) has an awareness of the universally valid moral norms. To every man this awareness is potentially given, even though actually distorted by culture, education, and his existential estrangement from his true being. This classical theory of natural law has only an indirect relation to the concept of physical laws, the laws of nature in the ordinary sense of the word. Natural law in our context is the law of moral reason or, as Kant calls it, "practical reason." For Stoic thought it has a common source with the physical laws in the divine *logos*, who is creatively present both in the laws of nature and in the natural moral laws of the human mind. Christianity accepted the Stoic doctrine, and most systems of religious thought have developed similar concepts. It is a general and unavoidable human problem, present in the quest for truth as well as in the demand for justice.

Its background is the awareness man has of the gap between what he essentially is, and therefore ought to be, and what he actually is, a consciousness of estrangement from and contradiction of his essential being. The emphasis on this estrangement by some radical Protestant thinkers has induced them to reject the theory of natural law completely. Man has totally lost what he essentially—or by creation—is. There is no knowledge of his true nature in him, unless it be given him by divine revelation. The revelation through man's created nature is veiled by his separation from God. A new revelatory experience is necessary, such as that which inspired the Mosaic law or the Sermon on the Mount.

But there is *self-deception* in every denial of the natural moral law. For those who deny it must admit that a divinely revealed moral law cannot contradict the divinely created human nature. It can only be a restatement of the law that is embodied in man's essential nature. And after having conceded this, these critics must go one step further toward affirming the doctrine of natural law. Man's essential nature cannot be lost as long as man is man. It can be distorted in the process of actualization, but it cannot disappear. The very statement that man is estranged from his created nature presupposes an experience of the abyss between what he essentially is and what he existentially is. Even a weak or misled conscience is still a conscience, namely, the silent voice of man's own essential nature, judging his actual being.

To defend the natural law theory against its religious critics is also to attack the nominalistic rejection of the idea of universal moral norms and its attempt to explain all ethical demands as expressions of social needs or of political power structures. If this were possible (which it is not), the concept of "man's essential nature" would have to be eliminated, and the experience of the conflict between what man essentially is and what he existentially is would have to be explained away. Undoubtedly, the concrete formulation of moral commands and their interpretation in ethical systems are largely conditioned by the social situation. But in all the varieties of cultures and religions and, consequently, of ethical systems, some basic norms appear. They are rooted in man's essential nature and ultimately in the structure of being itself. Their elaboration is the task of a developed theory of natural law. And here it might be added that such a theory underlies not only all ethical systems, but also all systems of "law" in the sense of jurisprudence.

The discussion of relativism has shown that basic ethical norms must unite an absolute element and a relative element. They must be universally valid and, at the same time, adaptable to the concrete situation. This tension appears conspicuously in the contrast between the Roman Catholic and a possible Protestant theory of natural law. The Roman Catholic theory asserts that it is possible to derive a considerable number of particular demands from certain universal principles through rational deduction. Such demands, if reached by sound methods of reasoning, are valid for all times and all situations. No revelatory event is necessary in order to discover them, and no change of the historical conditions can undercut their validity. There is, however, a point of uncertainty: those who analyze and deduce are human beings and, consequently, open to errors and distortions. Therefore, the church must decide what is the real natural law. Only the supranatural can confirm the validity of the natural, although the natural is true in itself. In this way the Catholic church has developed a system of natural moral laws which can be established and defended rationally, but which requires, because of human error, supranatural sanction by the church. The discussions regarding admissible methods of birth control or the educational authority of parents are actual examples.

Quite different is the Protestant attitude. Not much of a theory of natural law has been developed. This was partly due to the fact that Protestant biblicism attempted to derive ethical demands directly from the Bible, Calvinism particularly from the Old Testament. Another cause was the general Protestant distrust of reason, an implication of the doctrine of man's depravity in all parts of his nature, in mind as well as in body, in reason as well as in instincts. (The misleading term "total depravity" does not mean complete depravity, but estrangement from one's true being in *all* parts of one's actual being.) Finally, the Protestant principle denies that there can be any human institution, including a church with its doctrines and ethical demands, above the dynamics of history. A system of unchangeable laws of concrete morality contradicts the creative powers in life and spirit, and it contradicts the transforming work of the divine Spirit within and outside the church. Protestantism can accept the element of relativity in ethics and can develop with its help a dynamic doctrine of the natural moral law.

This, however, cannot be done without an answer to the question: is there a religious source of the moral demands? If so, how is it related to the formal answer given before, that the moral imperative demands that man become actually what he is essentially, a person within a community of persons? What does this mean concretely? What norms of moral action are implied in this demand? It will be necessary to answer these questions in sequence, and to build, step by step, a structure of moral action that embodies both the absolute and the relative, the static and the dynamic, the religious and the secular elements of ethical thought and moral experience.

First, let us examine the phrase "within a community of persons." Contemporary ethical theory has strongly emphasized the person-to-person encounter as the experiential root of morality. The decisive reason for this is the basic difference between the encounter of a person with another person and his encounter with nonpersonal realities (Martin Buber's ego-thou as opposed to ego-it). In the second case, man's encounter with nature outside him, for example, there is no limit in dealing with it. Man can make it into an object, dissect it, analyze it, or construct something new, a technical product, out of its parts or elements. Man can subject nature, progressively and almost limitlessly in all directions, to his knowledge and his action. The only limit is man's own finitude. But no one can actually establish this limit. Before it is reached nothing can resist man's cognitive and technical attack on nonpersonal reality. Nothing can resist man's will to transform it into an object and to use it for his purpose.

There is, however, a limit here and now in the ego-thou encounter. The limit is the other person. This seems a simple and obvious statement. But it is not so simple when we ask: where do we encounter a person? The answer—in every human being—is helpful only if we define living beings as human, if they are, according to their psychophysical structure, potential persons. This definition would include all degrees of the actualization of human potentiality, from the newborn child to the mature, wise man. But it does not determine which groups within the psychophysical species, human race, *have* the personal potential. Throughout human history this has been (and still is in some respects) undecided. Slaves, women, enemies, and special races were considered as objects with limited or unacknowledged humanity. And often children, the sick and old, the mentally abnormal and criminals were treated as mere objects, even though they belonged to a group whose personal potential was acknowledged, because they had not yet actualized or no longer were able to actualize their personal potential. This uncertainty with respect to beings who can be encountered as persons shows that the attempt to escape the relativities of history in the moral realm by formalizing the first principle cannot be successful. In the very moment the principle must be applied, traditions, conventions, and authorities, on the one hand, and criticism, decisions, and personal risk, on the other, determine the ethical demands.

Nevertheless, there are indications that man's essential nature makes itself heard in the midst of these uncertainties. Christianity, although it did not liberate slaves, gave them the status of potential persons by conceiving them as equal in their relation to God. And the Stoics, who achieved more than Christianity for political emancipation, did so in the name of the universal *logos* in which every human being participates. Both movements, and even earlier legislators who limited the arbitrary mistreatment of slaves, must have been aware of the fact that he who turns a human being (in the psychophysical sense) into a mere object suffers distortion of his own personal center. The same, of course, is true of the man who treats a woman as a mere object, or of a parent who deals with his child as though it were a thing, or of a tyrant who attempts to transform his subjects into tools for his purposes. They all become depersonalized themselves. Popular enlightenment in regard to these relationships has enlarged the circle of those considered potential persons. The circle in principle includes all human beings, although in reality it never does, even where the all-inclusive principle has been accepted, as, for example, in the racial conflict.

This discussion has led us to the deepest roots of what is usually called justice. All the implications of the idea of justice, especially the various forms of equality and liberty, are applications of the imperative to acknowledge every potential person as a person. Here, too, is the point at which every legal system of justice depends on some interpretation, consciously or unconsciously, of the moral idea of justice.

There is, however, a limit to the formulation of the moral principle of justice thus far. The acknowledgment of somebody as a person remains an external act that can be performed with legal detachment or cool objectivity. It can achieve justice without creating a relationship. Under many conditions this is the only way of actualizing justice, especially in encounters of social groups. But mere objectivity never occurs between human beings. Accompanying "pure" detachment is always an element of involvement. In the encounter of person with person within a community of persons, "community" also expresses involvement because it implies mutual participation, and, by participation, union. And the desire for union of the separated (which is ultimately *re*-union) is love. All communions are embodiments of love, the urge for participation in the other one. Justice is taken into love if the acknowledgment of the other person as person is not detached but involved. In this way, love becomes the ultimate moral principle, including justice and transcending it at the same time.

However, at this point it is necessary to combat several misinterpretations of the principle of love. First, it must be emphasized that if love takes justice into itself, justice is not diminished but enhanced. It has become creative justice in the sense of the Old and New Testament concepts of the *Yedaquah* and *Dikaiosyne* of God that both judges and saves. The frequent cry of Jews who have suffered immeasurable injustice through two millennia of church history—"We do not want love, we want justice"—is based on a misunderstanding of the biblical idea of love. Love, in the sense of *agape*, contains justice in itself as its unconditional element and as its weapon against its own sentimentalization. It is regrettable that Christianity has often concealed its unwillingness to do justice, or to fight for it, by setting off love against justice, and performing works of love in the sense of "charity" instead of battling for the removal of social injustice.

One of the reasons for this misunderstanding of love is the identification of love with emotion. Love, like every human experience, of course includes an emotional element, and this can in the case of love prove to be overwhelmingly strong. But this element is not the whole of love. Above all, love as *agape* is far removed from pity, although it can have elements of pity within a particular situation. Nietzsche's attack on the Christian idea of love is caused by this confusion. But it should serve to warn the Christian church to demonstrate in teaching, preaching, and liturgy the unconditional demand for justice in the very nature of *agape*. (I believe it would be salutary if the word "love" in the sense of *agape* could be avoided for a long time, and the word *agape* introduced into modern language.)

Agape is a quality of love, that quality which expresses the self-transcendence of the religious element in love. If love is the ultimate norm of all moral demands, its *agape* quality points to the transcendent source of the content of the moral imperative. For *agape* transcends the finite possibilities of man. Paul indicates this in his great hymn to love (I Corinthians 13) when he describes *agape* as the highest work of the divine Spirit, and as an element of the eternal life, even beyond faith and hope.

Agape as the self-transcending element of love is not separated from the other elements that usually are described as *epithymia*—the *libido* quality of love, *philia*—the friendship quality of love, and *eros*—the mystical quality of love. In all of them what we have called "the urge toward the reunion of the separated" is effective, and all of them stand under the judgment of *agape*. For love is one, even if one of its qualities predominates. None of the qualities is ever completely absent. There is, for example, the compassion element of *philia* and *eros* in *agape*, and there is the *agape* quality in genuine compassion (a fact important for the dialogue between Christianity and Buddhism). It is this *agape* element that prevents participation in the other one from becoming mere identification with him, as compassion prevents *agape* from becoming a detached act of mere obedience to the "law of love." And there is *eros* in *agape*, and *agape* in *eros*, a fact that permitted Christianity to receive into itself the *eros*-created classical culture, both rational and mystical. It is the *agape* element in *eros* that prevents culture from becoming a nonserious, merely transitory entertainment, just as *eros* prevents *agape* from becoming a moralistic turning away from the creative potentialities in nature and man toward an exclusive commitment to a God who can only be feared or obeyed, but not loved. For without *eros* toward the ultimate good there is no love toward God. Even the libidinous quality of love is always present in the highest forms of *eros, philia,* and *agape.* Man is a multidimensional unity and not a composite of parts.* Therefore, all elements of man's being participate in every moral decision and action.

On this basis we may judge asceticism in the light of the principle of *agape.* First, nothing created is bad in itself. Matter is not an antidivine principle from which the "soul" has to be liberated. The desire for union with material reality through the senses is an expression of love as *libido.* And in *libido,* elements of *eros, philia,* and *agape* are present, as *libido* is present in them. As in all other instances, the problem is how much *agape* is effective in the *libido* drives of love —in the desire for food, drink, sex, and aesthetic enjoyment. If the *libido* quality overpowers the *agape* element, and with it also the *eros* and *philia* elements, resistance in the name of *agape* is necessary and, under some conditions, partial or total asceticism with respect to things that are in themselves good. This "disciplinary" asceticism is quite different from the "ontological" asceticism which avoids things because of the material element in them. The former is affirmed by *agape,* the latter rejected by it.

This distinction applies also to the ecstatic element of religion which has a definite psychosomatic dimension in unity with its spiritual dimension. The union of these two factors characterizes every genuine ecstasy, including every serious prayer that reaches to the divine Presence. The *libido* element in love prevents *agape* from becoming a rational

* These ideas are fully elaborated in the first section of the third volume of my *Systematic Theology* (Chicago: University of Chicago Press, 1963), under the heading, "Life and the Spirit."

calculation of how to give the best possible help to others, as the *agape* element in love prevents *libido* from running wild and destroying the centered person, and with it the power of *eros* and *philia*.

Love is one. Its different qualities belong to each other, although they may become isolated and antagonistic toward each other. Decisive in all situations is *agape*, because it is united with justice and transcends the finite limits of human love. Therefore, in any conflict of the qualities of love, *agape* is the determining element. Only on this basis can love be called the ultimate source of moral demands. If love is understood in this way a second answer to the question of religion and morality is provided. The first was the unconditional character of the moral imperative. The second is the transcendent character of the ultimate source of moral demands— love under the dominance of *agape*. This again demonstrates that morality has a religious quality even when independent of any system of ethics that belongs to a religion in the narrower sense of the word.

In calling love the source of moral norms we have answered the first question of this chapter, namely, that of the relativity of ethics. For love is both absolute and relative by its very nature. An unchanging principle, it nevertheless always changes in its concrete application. It "listens" to the particular situation. Abstract justice cannot do this; but justice taken into love and becoming "creative justice" or *agape* can do so. *Agape* acts in relation to the concrete demands of the situation—its conditions, its possible consequences, the inner status of the people involved, their hidden motives, their limiting complexes, and their unconscious desires and anxieties. Love perceives all these—and more deeply the stronger the *agape* element is. (In line with this thought we might interject that the discovery of the psychology of the unconscious was a work not only of creative *eros*, but also of creative justice or *agape,* in spite of the antireligious bias of many representatives of the psychoanalytic movement.)

Christian theology has dealt with the problem of the concrete moral decision in terms of the doctrine of the divine Spirit. The "Spiritual Presence," the presence of the divine Ground of Being toward and in the human spirit, opens man's eyes and ears to the moral demand implicit in the concrete situation. Tables of laws can never wholly apply to the unique situation. This is true of the Ten Commandments as well as of the demands of the Sermon on the Mount and the moral prescriptions in the Epistles of Paul. "The letter kills" not only because it judges him who cannot fulfill the law, but because it suppresses the creative potentialities of the unique moment which never was before and never will come again. The Spirit, on the contrary, opens the mind to these potentialities and determines the decisions of love in a particular situation. In this way the problem of the absolute and the relative character of the moral demands is solved in principle. Love, as the ultimate principle of morality, is always the same. Love entering the unique situation, in the power of the Spirit, is always different. Therefore love liberates us from the bondage to absolute ethical traditions, to conventional morals, and to authorities that claim to know the right decision perhaps without having listened to the demand of the unique moment. The Spirit is the Spirit of newness. It breaks the prison of any absolute moral law, even when vested with the authority of a sacred tradition. Love can reject as well as utilize every moral tradition, and it always scrutinizes the validity of a moral convention. But love itself cannot question itself and it cannot be questioned by anything else.

The problem of this chapter—the religious source of the moral demands—has so far been answered in three statements concerning the ultimate principle of ethical norms. The first statement referred to the idea of justice, the affirmation of every person as a person. The second described love, taking justice into itself, as the ultimate principle of moral demands. And the third pointed to the dependence of moral demands on the concrete situation in its uniqueness.

There is, however, one unanswered question, namely, what is the function of the formulated laws for moral action? They appear abundantly in sacred texts that consecrate them and provide them with an almost unconditional validity. We must now ask: what is their significance within the structure developed up to this point? The answer lies in the word "wisdom." They represent the wisdom of the past about man, his relation to others and to himself, his predicament in temporal existence, and the *telos* or inner aim of his being. Wisdom, in the later centuries of the ancient world, became (like *logos*) a divine power, mediating between God and the world and between God and man. It was (again like *logos*) a principle of the divine self-manifestation in nature and history. According to the book of Job, God made the world while looking at "Wisdom" which was beside Him. In history it has inspired men and showed them the right way; it has had revelatory power and it became embodied in Jesus as the Christ. Wisdom, in this sense, is the source of the tables of laws in many religions and cultures. From the point of view of man, revelations, mediated by wisdom, are the result of both accumulated experience and revelatory visions. As such, they are of tremendous weight, but do not possess unconditional validity. They guide the conscience in concrete situations, but none of them, taken as law, has absolute validity. Even the Ten Commandments express not only man's essential nature but also the wisdom and the limitations of an early feudal culture. Certainly there is risk in deviating from the wisdom embodied in a concrete tradition. But there is also risk in accepting a tradition without questioning it. The former is an external and an internal risk, the latter only an internal risk. The former brings isolation and attack, the latter safety and praise. But accepting or trespassing traditional morals is spiritually justified only if done with self-scrutiny, often in the pain of a split conscience, and with the courage to decide even when the risk of error is involved. (See Chapter IV.)

Most human beings follow the guidance of the moral tradition when they obey the moral imperative. Everyone needs such guidance for his daily life and its innumerable large and small ethical questions. A considerable amount of moral habit is necessary in order to fulfill the demands of an average existence. Therefore, the tables of laws, which are commandments of the divine-human wisdom of all generations, are gifts of grace, although they can become destructive when elevated to absolute validity and substituted for *agape* and its power to listen to the voice of the "now."

One might ask: is love also the ultimate principle for social ethics? And we must answer affirmatively, because the encounter of social groups is an encounter in which reunion of the separated is the *telos*, just as it is in the person-to-person encounter. But there is a decisive difference. Social groups are power groups with no personal center. They have a changing organizational center in terms of their government. But they have no personal center. This means that there are great differences in the way love is effective in social ethics. Any attempt to identify the problems of personal ethics and social ethics (as does legalistic pacifism, for example) ignores the reality of power in the social realm, and so confuses the organizational centeredness of a historical group with the personal centeredness of a person. A discussion of the problems indicated by this statement requires the development of a philosophy of power. This we cannot do within the framework of the present study.*

To summarize the thesis of this chapter: the religious source of the moral demands is love under the domination of its *agape* quality, in unity with the imperative of justice to acknowledge every being with personal potential as a person, being guided by the divine-human wisdom embodied in the moral laws of the past, listening to the concrete situation, and acting courageously on the basis of these principles.

Out of such decisions in the power of love new insights would grow. And they might transform the given tables of laws into something more adequate for our situation as a whole as well as for innumerable individual situations. Should this occur, love as the ultimate principle of the moral demands would be powerfully vindicated.

* But I have developed such a philosophy in my volume *Love, Power and Justice.*

III

The Religious Element
in Moral Motivation

After having discovered its religious dimension in the unconditional character of the moral imperative, and the religious
source of the moral demands under the dominance of *agape,*
we now must ask whether there is a religious element in the
process of moral motivation.

The question leads immediately to the concept of law. The
unconditional moral imperative confronts us as the sacred
moral law. It appears as the only justifiable motivation. Any
other motivation would seem to introduce conditions that
violate the unconditional character of morality. This is the
basic point of view of Kant's rigoristic (not Puritan or Pietist)
ethical theory. It would reduce the religious element in
morality to the unconditional character of the moral imperative. We have already trespassed against this restriction
with respect to the source of the ethical demands by establishing love as this source, without surrendering the formal strict-
ness of the Kantian principles. We must now do likewise with
respect to moral motivation.

As the linguistic form itself indicates, the moral imperative
has the form of a commandment and, if generalized, a law.
We have discussed the term "law" in connection with the
natural laws of morals, and distinguished it from the physical
laws of nature. This difference extensively influences the

problem of moral motivation: the moral law is experienced as law only because man is estranged from the structural law of his essential being, namely, to become a centered person. This law belongs to him. It is his nature. And it would never become a commanding law if he did not try to break through it. But if he is estranged from it, if he contradicts it in his existence, it becomes law for him. And since all human beings share this predicament, they all stand under the law. And even love becomes law for them—"Thou shalt love . . ." If love determined our being, if it were a structural law with which we were one, it could not become a law that commands or an expression of the moral imperative. It would be an expression of our being, one with it, and not standing in opposition to it.

We can use this understanding of the law as a key to two biblical stories of great symbolic power—one, the temptation of Adam, and the other, the temptation of the Christ. In the story of the Fall, God forbids Adam to eat from the tree of knowledge (which is also power). We ask: why is this prohibition necessary? If Adam had been one with his true being, the negative command would not have been necessary. But as a man, he had the freedom to contradict his true being. In his condition of temptation he had not yet done so, but the tendency was in him, which means that he was already separated from the natural unity with God. The law appeared when the first symptoms of separation appeared, and the innocence of the created state of being in God was shaken. The law was a warning, a summoning back to original innocence. But by this very fact the innocence was no longer innocence. Neither was it guilt. It was on the boundary line of both, and the name of this boundary line is "desire."

This analysis of innocence, desire, and law can also be applied to one of the most problematic stories of the Gospels, the story of the temptations of Jesus. Some theologians deny the seriousness of the temptations; others affirm it, but are not aware of the consequences of their affirmation. In declaring with the New Testament and most classical theology the seriousness of the temptations of Jesus, we must acknowledge that they are expressions of his true humanity. They should have protected his image against the seemingly irrepressible Monophysitic trends in all Christian churches—that is, against the theological error strongly supported by popular piety, which is to see in Jesus *a* god, walking on earth. But if the temptations of Jesus are taken seriously, the question arises whether their seriousness presupposes a separation from that unity with God that determines his whole life and makes him the selected "Son." The question can be answered by reference to the Adam story. Serious temptation presupposes desire for that by which one is tempted. Jesus, like Adam, stood between innocence and guilt, on the boundary line of existence where the commanding law appears. And Jesus quotes commanding words from the Old Testament against Satan.

With this insight into the two different meanings of law, law as structure and law as the demand to actualize this structure, we approach the question: has the law in the second sense a motivating power for the fulfillment of the moral imperative and its concrete demands? The answer, like the answer to the question of the ultimate principle of the content of morality, must be developed along several levels. For it is complex, representing the profoundest tensions in religious experience and in the history of Christianity.

The general question is: can the commanding law, which presupposes the contrast between our essential and our actual being, motivate us to transform ourselves in the direction of reuniting the actual with the essential? The first logically consistent answer: it *cannot!* For the very existence of the commanding law is based on that split. The law (in the following sections used only in the sense of the commanding law) is an expression of man's estrangement from his true nature. How would it then be able to overcome this estrangement? This logically unavoidable answer is also the psychologically experienced answer: The command to be good does not make us good. It may indeed drive us toward evil!

Let us consider this answer in several realms of experience. Most contemporary is the psychotherapeutic discovery that the least effective way of treating a person under a destructive compulsion—alcoholism, for example—is to direct him in terms of a moral command, "Don't drink any more!" No psychoanalyst worthy of his profession would commit this destructive error. The law, as stated by the analyst, would produce a tremendous resistance in the patient, and justly so. The patient would withdraw to his freedom to contradict himself, even though he might then destroy himself. The patient, in this action, defends a decisive element in human freedom. Psychoanalysts who (according to the latest fashion) begin to moralize to their patients, however cautiously, should remember that it is precisely the pathological loss of power to respond to moral commands that makes these persons patients. Most analysts are still conscious of this, preserving one of the deepest insights of psychotherapy, namely, that the law cannot break compulsions, that the "thou shalt" does not liberate. Instead of encountering the law, the patient encounters acceptance on the part of the effective analyst. He is accepted in the state in which he is, and he is not told to change his state before becoming acceptable. In some cases, especially in pre-analytic counseling, the acceptance can express itself in a description by the counselor of how he himself was or still remains in a similar predicament, so that he ceases to be merely the subject, and the patient merely the object, in the healer-patient relationship.

One has accused psychotherapy of permissiveness. In particular cases this criticism is just—formerly, even more so. But so far as the method is concerned, this permissiveness is a result of a simple confusion between acceptance and permission. In the analytic situation there is neither command nor permission, but acceptance and healing. If the power of the compulsion is broken, a counseling exchange between the healer and the healed may take place, and the question may arise as to what the patient should do with his newly regained freedom. Only then should the problems of morality, its content, and its motivation come into focus, and the analyst may become a friend or a priest to the patient. But then the further question for both of them must be raised whether the moral law, appealing to their freedom, has motivating power, or whether it is powerless without a religious element in it— the religious element being an acceptance that transcends the psychotherapeutic distinction between the healer and healed.

Another relationship in which the question of the motivating power of the law is decisive is the educational one, first within the family, and then in the school and any other situation where an educational element is implied. There are many problems connected with the motivating power of the law in the educational realm. First, it is necessary to distinguish between demands based on authority and demands based on rationality. The distinction is rarely absolute because there is always authority behind educational demands; and this authority always claims to be rational. Nevertheless, it makes a great difference to the child, if he can understand a parental order as adequate to the situation, or if he feels it as a mere exercise of incomprehensible authority. In either case the child may resist. But in the first, the resistance is not rebellious; it is a primitive form of self-affirmation, weakened by a subconscious acknowledgment that the order was justified. Then the essential nature of the child is partly united with the content of the command, and to the degree to which it is united, the order proves not to be a strange law imposed by adult authority, but an expression of the demand of a practical situation, such as the necessary regulation of hours at home and in school. Therefore, it is of great importance to the educational process to help the child to understand the objective validity of the orders he receives.

If this is not accomplished, or if the orders themselves are more the expressions of willful authority than of the situation, the child is driven toward a genuine rebellion, and three things can happen: the rebellion may succeed and a creative independence develop; or the rebellion may succeed externally but fail internally, and rebelliousness as a character trait may result; or the rebellion may fail externally and internally, leaving a broken, submissive character. These examples show the problem of the law in a realm where it is almost daily experienced, and where parents, teachers, and even philosophers of education, have concluded that the law should be removed altogether and replaced by a kind of organized permissiveness. This, however, has led to consequences in which the "dialectics of the law" are patently manifest. After a certain time (usually in later adolescence), the majority of children become well-adapted conformists, albeit on a superficial level. Those among them who feel this superficiality as emptiness complain that they never had to face the law seriously and remained without guidance to their own essential nature and its potentialities. In view of this situation one must agree with the apostle who was most critical of the commanding law—Paul—that "the law is good," for it expresses the created goodness of man, which man must face because he is estranged from it.

The reference to Paul leads to the realm in which the problem of moral motivation and, consequently, of the motivating power of the law, has been experienced and discussed most thoroughly and most profoundly in religion and theology. It is not the general question of the religious element

in the moral motivation that concerns us at this moment, but
the attitude toward the law in some of the greatest religious
men. Their experience is not restricted to religion in the
narrower sense of the word, but is typical of human experience
generally. There is no text in theology, philosophy, and psychology that deals more profoundly with the problem of the
law than the seventh chapter of Paul's Letter to the Romans.
He praises the law as "holy in itself" and the commandment
as "holy and just and good." He calls it "spiritual." In his
"inmost self" he "delights in the law of God," he is "subject
to God's law as a rational being." Without the law he would
"never have become acquainted with sin." This is one facet
of Paul's evaluation of the law: the law is the expression of
what man essentially is and therefore ought to be, but what he
actually is *not,* as the law shows to him.

The other side of Paul's evaluation of the law is based on
his experience that the law commands us to do the good that
we cannot do because we are estranged from it and under a
power that contradicts our true being: "Clearly, it is no
longer I who am the agent, but sin that has its lodging in me."
But the law does more than show us our essential nature and
our estrangement from it. The law awakens the sleeping sin:
"In the absence of law, sin is a dead thing"; "When the commandment came sin sprang to life"; "Through the commandment, sin became more sinful than ever." It is obvious that
Paul does not consider the law as a power of moral motivation. He was, on the basis of his own experience, aware of
the fact that the commanding law produces "all kinds of
wrong desires," but does not motivate the conquest of these
desires and the reunion of his actual will with his essential
will: "What I do is the wrong which is against my will."

Paul's experience is independent of the religious framework
in which it appears. A humanist with insight into his spiritual
predicament could fully agree with it. Actually, however, and

not by chance, the problem of the law as motivating power appeared again in its profundity and explosive power in the Protestant Reformation. All Reformers fought the idea that man's "good works," his fulfillment of the law, could be a contributing factor in salvation, or the acceptance of man by God. Not the fulfillment of commandments (which is impossible in the state of separation from God), but the acceptance of the message that we are accepted, is the motive of moral action. Nevertheless, the Reformers maintained a threefold use of the law—first, in its legal function as the principle of the postive law, the law of the nations; second, in its power to awaken our conscience to the fact that our actual existence contradicts our essential being, that we are estranged from ourselves; and third, in its function as a mirror of what is good and bad in Christian life. Luther denied and Calvin affirmed the third function of the law. But all the Reformers denied its power of moral motivation.

Again it was a personal experience, namely, that of Luther, that led to the rediscovery of Paul's experience and its theological implications. The depth to which Luther felt the ambiguity of the law emerges in expressions of hate, not only against the law itself, but also against the image of God who lays down a law nobody can fulfill and who punishes those who trespass against it. The shaking anxiety produced by this thought, and the hidden hatred against God, break out in Luther repeatedly, even in his later period. In such a state of mind, man is not able to recognize the law as the expression of his own essential being; he feels it as a strange and tyrannical command. But as with Paul, this is not Luther's sole evaluation of the law. The interpretation of the Ten Commandments in Luther's *Small Catechism* demonstrates that he is able to see in the law the right expression of man's relation to God and man in such a way that the right relation to God —love and fear—provides the moral motivation. Beyond this,

his interpretation indicates, as for every table of laws, a particular situation—in this case the paternalistic kind of rural society in which he lived. (Cf. Chapter II.)

The ambiguity of the commanding law, as experienced by Luther, was the decisive problem for the entire period of the Reformation. The emphasis was different in different Reformers, but the basic answer was the same. The enormous tension produced by this ambiguity, however, slowly receded, and Protestantism became to a large extent a religion of the law, doctrinal as well as moral.

All systems, determined by the law, whether religious or secular, are systems of compromise. This is true of groups as well as of individuals; and it is true of the great majority of human beings and human situations in all periods. This happens because the moral law becomes embodied in state law, conventional rules, and educational principles (with or without the support of a particular religion), and exercises motivating power through tradition, public opinion, personal habit, and the threats and promises connected with all of them. In this way the commanding law has the power to produce moral action in an institutionalized form. It is, generally speaking, what the Reformers called the "first use of the law," its power to produce "civil justice," since obedience to the laws makes the existence of society possible. From the point of view of the unconditional moral imperative, and love as the ultimate principle of moral commands, these methods of motivating moral action are compromises, unavoidable in view of the human predicament, but far removed from the true nature of the moral. This is true not only because of the universal human estrangement, the struggle between man's essential and existential nature, the ambiguity of good and evil in every life process, the mixture of moral and amoral motives in every moral act, but also because social institutions as well as personal habits have an almost irresistible tendency to perpetuate themselves in disregard of the demands of creative justice in a new situation or under unique conditions, both in the communal and in the individual life. To summarize: the law provides moral motivation if morality becomes a thread within a texture of premoral forces and motives.

To acknowledge this aspect of man's predicament is an act of humility, demanded by honest self-evaluation. But this demand is not fulfilled by most people. They evaluate their highly ambiguous moral achievements as sufficiently perfect, morally speaking; and there are even some who evaluate them as expressions of the nearly perfect or most perfect moral fulfillment. They consider themselves as "moral men," or as "men of good will," and look down on those who are "immoral men" or who at least do not belong to the selected group of the "men of good will." They do not see the ambiguity of their goodness and the mixture of their motives. They are not hypocritical, but self-assured in their high moral standing. They do not feel that they need forgiveness, either in Christian or in humanist terms. They defend the motivating power of the moral law, pointing to themselves as examples.

But some of these "moral men" and some of the "immoral men" are, at some point, grasped by the unconditional seriousness of the moral imperative, and they then recognize its deep opposition to them, even to the best qualities in them. This experience unites Paul the "righteous Pharisee," and Augustine the "sinner," and Luther the "ascetic monk." They took the moral imperative without compromise and without self-deception, and concluded that the "naked" moral law has no motivating power. They looked for something that had this power, and they found it in the religious element which they called "grace," a word that requires much interpretation to become an answer also for us.

But before discussing grace as the power of moral motivation, I should like to recall two concepts which belong together and represent the highest levels that Greek humanism reached in solving the question of moral motivation, and which remain decisive for the amalgamation of the moral with the cultural.

One is classically expressed by Socrates when he speaks of the knowing of the good, which creates the doing of the good. The question, of course, is: what kind of knowledge can create moral action? It is immediately clear that it cannot be the detached knowledge of prescientific or scientific inquiry, nor can it be the practical knowledge of the day-to-day handling of things and people, even if such knowledge is elevated to the level of technical expertise or psychological skill, for any of this can be used for the performance of the most anti-moral actions. (Our most flagrant modern example of this is the Nazi system.) Since we cannot assume, unlike some of his critics, that Socrates was cognizant of this danger, we must search for another kind of knowledge he might have had in mind. Perhaps we approximate it when we use the modern term "insight." If Socrates did mean "insight," he stands in line with his great predecessors—for example, Heraclitus and Parmenides. Heraclitus' attack against those who are "fools" is not a criticism of the unsophisticated, but of those not subject to the power of the *logos*, the universal law of things and mind, the source of the physical and moral laws. Those who are not grasped by the *logos* are fools, and he directs his prophetic-philosophical wrath against them. In this way he established the idea of the wise man who unites knowledge with personal involvement in the universal *logos*, an idea which became of immense practical significance in the humanist-religious philosophy of the Stoics. Wisdom became the leading virtue in the later ancient world, combining cognition and morality.

Knowledge of the character of wisdom cannot be considered

as functioning in one direction only, as the cause of moral action, because it is in itself partly a result of moral action. Since one must be good in order to be wise, goodness is not a consequence of wisdom. The Socratic assertion, therefore, that knowledge creates virtue must be interpreted as knowledge in which the whole person is involved (insight). That is, a cognitive act which is united with a moral act can cause further moral acts (and further cognition).

It is worthwhile to look, in addition to the Heraclitean-Stoic tradition, to that of Parmenides and the Gospel of John. In the philosophical poem about being and nonbeing, Parmenides describes the visionary experience in which the goddess of justice (!) opens his eyes to the true way of asking the ultimate questions. He derives his insight from a kind of revelatory act which takes away his blindness to the truth, and guides him not to a better method of research (although this is an important consequence of his insight), but to a way of life as a whole. In the Fourth Gospel we also find passages in which truth is being. Jesus says, "I *am* the truth." There are others which state that truth can be done, those who do the truth will recognize the truth. Here the gap between the cognitive and the moral is conquered, and again it is obvious that this kind of insight cannot precede the moral act and motivate it, since it is itself partly a moral act.

A modern analogy to these ideas is provided by the psychotherapeutic experience. It clearly shows the difference between detached knowledge and participating insight. No one is helped in his personal problems by a thorough knowledge of the psychoanalytic literature. On the contrary, the analyst knows that a patient who claims to have insight into his own pathological state on the basis of such knowledge deceives himself, and often sets up an almost insuperable resistance against gaining true insight about himself. Only he who enters the healing process with his whole being, cognitive as well as moral, and therefore with emotional attachment to the process and its different elements, has a chance of gaining healing. But this cannot occur without a "walk through hell," the suffering implicit in the awareness of the dark, ordinarily repressed elements in our being. Here also, the moral change is only partly an effect of insight, as insight itself is partly an effect of the moral will to be liberated.

There is another concept by which classical Greek humanism attempted to answer the question of moral motivation. It is the concept of *eros* as used by Plato. In the second chapter we defined it as the mystical quality of love. This description of *eros* depends both on Plato's use of the word in the *Symposium* and on the reintroduction of the word into Christian mysticism by Dionysios the Areopagite. *Eros* for Plato is a mediating power, elevating the human mind out of existential bondage into the realm of pure essences, and finally to the essence of all essences—the idea of the good that is, at the same time, the idea of the beautiful and the true. As in the other examples of Greek tradition, the moral and the cognitive are not separate. *Eros* provides both insight and moral motivation, and there is a third element, the aesthetic desire for the beautiful which is implied in the good. This goal can be attained by *eros* as a divine-human power that transcends the moral command without denying it. *Eros* is the transmoral motivation for moral action.

To be impelled by *eros* can also be described as being grasped by that toward which *eros* drives. And thus we return to the principle of love, as discussed in the second chapter. It is one of the qualities of love that concerns us here—the mystical, the drive toward reunion with essential being in everything, ultimately with the good as the principle of being and knowing (in Platonic terms). Love in all its qualities drives toward reunion. *Eros*, as distinct from *philia* and *libido,* drives toward reunion with things and persons in their essential goodness and with the good itself. For mystical theology, God and the good itself are identical; therefore the love toward the good itself is, in religious language, love toward God. This love can be symbolized in two ways: in Plato it is the divine-human power of *eros* that elevates the mind to the divine; and in Aristotle, it is the power of the divine that attracts every finite thing and produces by this attraction the movement of the stars, the universe, and the human mind.

According to both formulations it is not the moral imperative in its commanding majesty and strangeness that is morally motivating, but the driving or attracting power of that which is the goal of the moral command—the good. The Greeks were aware of the fact that the moral realm, in the sense of personal and communal justice, does not furnish moral motivation unless it is understood as a station on the way to something ultimate in being and meaning—the divine. And the aim of everything finite is to participate in the life of the divine. The moral stage is a station on the way, and the motivation for it depends on the motivation for the transmoral aim, the participation in the divine life, as Aristotle expresses it both rationally and symbolically. These are the forms in which Greek humanism and its ethical thought expressed, in mystical-religious terms, the transmoral motivation of morality.

Again I should like to point out a contemporary analogy in the realm of therapeutic psychology. The question is whether *libido* is unlimited in itself or only under the conditions of human estrangement. Our line of thought decides for the latter (as opposed to Freud and his doctrine of the essential necessity of cultural uneasiness and the death-drive). The difference is that essential *libido* (toward food or sex, for example) is concretely directed to a particular object and is satisfied in the union with it, while existentially distorted *libido* is directed to the pleasure which may be derived from the relation to any encountered object. This drives existential *libido* boundlessly from object to object, while the essential *libido* is fulfilled if union with a particular object is achieved. This distinguishes the lover from the "Don Juan," and *agape*-directed *libido* from undirected *libido*. The moral imperative cannot be obeyed by a repression of *libido*, but only by the power of *agape* to control *libido* and to take it into itself as an element.

Eros is a divine-human power. It cannot be produced at will. It has the character of *charis, gratia,* "grace"—that which is given without prior merit and makes graceful him to whom it is given. It is useful to remember the origins of the word "grace," because it plays an immense role in Christian religion and theology, and its meaning and relevance have become incomprehensible for most contemporaries both inside and outside the church. Graces are divine gifts, independent of human merit, but dependent on the human readiness to receive them. And the readiness itself is the first gift of grace, which can be either preserved or lost.

Theology has distinguished between "common" grace that works in all realms of life and in all human relations, and the special grace bestowed upon those who are grasped by the new reality that has appeared in the Christ. In both respects, the problem of moral motivation is decisive. What common and special grace accomplish is to create a state of reunion in which the cleavage between our true and our actual being is fragmentarily overcome, and the rule of the commanding law is broken.

Where there is grace there is no command and no struggle to obey the command. This is true of all realms of life. He who has the grace of loving a thing, a task, a person, or an idea does not need to be asked to love, whatever quality of love may be predominant in his love. A reunion of something separated has already taken place, and with it a partial fulfillment of the moral imperative. As a gift of grace, it is not produced by one's will and one's endeavor. One simply receives it. In this sense we may say: there is grace in every reunion of being with being, insofar as it *is* reunion and not the misuse of the one by the other, insofar as justice is not violated.

Elements of grace permeate everyone's life. One could also call them healing powers that overcome the split between what we essentially are and what we actually are, and with this split the estrangement of life from life and the hidden or open hostility of life against life. Whenever elements of grace appear, the moral command is fulfilled. What was demanded, now is given. But what was given can be lost. And it will be lost, if one forgets that grace fulfills what the moral imperative demands, and that it affirms and does not replace the unconditional seriousness of morality. Therefore, as soon as grace is lost, the commanding law takes over and produces the painful experience of being unable to become what one could and should have become.

This suffering under the moral law finally drives us to the question of the meaning of our existence in the light of the unconditional moral command which cuts into our finite and estranged predicament. We feel that the many gifts of common grace do not suffice; we ask for a grace as unconditional as the moral imperative and as infinite as our failure to fulfill it. We ask for the religious element of moral motivation directly, after we have experienced its indirect effect as common grace in the different realms of life.

The Christian message is above all a message of grace. There is no religion without this element. The Old Testament, where the law plays such a decisive role, refers in every part to the divine covenant between God and the selected nation, and to the promises beyond all threats and judgments. We might cite similar examples from many other religions. But Christianity, particularly under the impact of the Protestant Reformation, has emphasized the idea of grace more than any other religion. The concept of grace in Christian thought contains a polarity between the element of forgiveness and the element of fulfillment. The former can be expressed as the forgiveness of sins or—in a paradoxical phrase—the acceptance of the unacceptable. The latter can be described as the gift of the Spirit or the infusion of love controlled by *agape*. The former conquers the pain of morally unfulfilled existence, and the latter grants the blessedness of an at least fragmentary fulfillment. Neither is possible without the other, for only he who is grasped by the Spirit can accept the tremendous paradox that he is accepted. Nothing is more difficult than to face one's image in the mirror of the law and to say "yes" to it in terms of "in spite of." It demands much grace to reach this state. And on the other hand, the fragmentary fulfillment through grace can bestow blessedness only if the paradox of forgiveness conquers the pain of missing fulfillment or of lost grace.

Here the skeptical question may arise as to whether the paradox of grace diminishes the power of moral motivation in those who accept that they are accepted, although unacceptable. It is a very old question, used against Paul as well as against Augustine, against Luther as well as against Calvin, and against the Reformation as a whole by the humanists and the evangelical radicals. It is a justified question insofar as it points to the possibility of converting the paradox of grace into a cover for lawlessness. But the question is not justified in principle, because it shows that one has not understood that the courage to accept the unacceptable is a work of grace, a creation of the Spiritual power. Only if the acceptance of the unacceptable is misunderstood as a merely intellectual act does it remain without moral motivating power. Orthodoxy (in contrast to the early Luther) is largely responsible for this intellectual distortion of the paradox of acceptance of the unacceptable and, consequently, for the attacks on the Pauline principles in the name of morality.

The question of moral motivation can be answered only transmorally. For the law demands, but cannot forgive; it judges, but cannot accept. Therefore, forgiveness and acceptance, the conditions of the fulfillment of the law, must come from something above the law, or more precisely, from something in which the split between our essential being and our existence is overcome and healing power has appeared. It is the center of the Christian message that this conquest took place in the Christ, in whom a new reality beyond the cleavage appeared. It is therefore a moralistic distortion of Christianity to interpret the so-called "teachings of Jesus" as another law, heavier than the law of Moses. His words (not his "teachings") point the way to the new reality in which the law is not abolished, but has ceased to be commanding.

The first three chapters of this volume have sought to demonstrate that the relation of religion and morality is not an external one, but that the religious dimension, source, and motivation are implicit in all morality, acknowledged or not. Morality does not depend on any concrete religion; it is religious in its very essence. The unconditional character of the moral imperative, love as the ultimate source of the moral commands, and grace as the power of moral motivation are the concepts through which the question of the relation of religion and morality is fundamentally answered.

IV

The Transmoral Conscience

In this chapter I shall discuss the transmoral conscience. The theologian Richard Rothe, in *Christian Ethics,* has made the suggestion that the word "conscience" be excluded from all scientific treatment of ethics, since its connotations are so manifold and contradictory that the term can no longer be usefully defined. If we look not only at the popular use of the word, with its complete lack of clarity, but also at its confused history, this desperate advice is understandable. Understandable as it may be, we should not follow it, for the word "conscience" points to a definite reality which, in spite of its complexity, can and must be described adequately. And the history of the idea of conscience, despite the bewildering variety of interpretations that it has produced, shows some clear types and definite trends.

The complexity of the phenomenon called "conscience" becomes apparent as soon as we look at the manifold problems it has given to human thought; man always and everywhere demonstrates something like a conscience, but its contents are subject to a continuous change. What is the relation between the form and the content of conscience? Conscience points to an objective structure of demands that make themselves perceivable through it, and represents, at the same time, the most subjective self-interpretation of personal life. What is the relation between the objective and the subjective sides of conscience? Conscience is an ethical concept, but it has a basic significance for religion. What is the relation between the ethical and the religious meaning of conscience? Conscience has many different functions; it is good or bad, commanding or warning, elevating or condemning, battling or indifferent. Which of these functions are basic, which derived? These questions refer only to the description of the phenomenon, not to its explanation or evaluation. They show its complex character and the reason for its confused history.

The concept of conscience is a creation of the Greek and Roman spirit. Wherever this spirit has been influential, notably in Christianity, conscience is a significant notion. The basic Greek word *syneidenai* ("knowing with," i.e., with oneself; "being witness of oneself") was common in popular language long before the philosophers utilized it. It described the act of observing oneself, often as judging oneself. In philosophical terminology it received the meaning of "self-consciousness" (for instance, in Stoicism, the derived substantives *syneidesis, synesis*). Philo of Alexandria, under the influence of the Old Testament, stressed the ethical self-observation in *syneidesis* and attributed to it the function of *elenchos,* that is, accusation and conviction. The Roman language, following the popular Greek usage, united the theoretical and practical emphasis, in the word *conscientia,* while philosophers like Cicero and Seneca admitted it to the ethical sphere and interpreted it as the trial of oneself, in accusation as well as in defense. In modern languages the theoretical and the practical aspects are usually expressed by different words. English distinguishes *consciousness* from *conscience;* German, *Bewusstsein* from *Gewissen;* French, *connaissance* from *conscience* (although the latter word is also used for the theoretical aspect).

The development of the reality as well as of the concept of conscience is connected with the breakdown of primitive conformism in a situation that forces the individual to face himself as such. In the sphere of an unbroken we-consciousness, no individual conscience can appear. Cultural phenomena such as Greek tragedy, with its emphasis on personal guilt and personal purification, or in later Judaism, the stress upon personal responsibility before God, prepared for the rise of conscience by creating a definite ego-consciousness. The self, says a modern philosopher, has been discovered by sin. The merely logical self-consciousness does not have such a power. Without practical knowledge about oneself, produced by the experience of law and guilt, no practical self-consciousness and no conscience could have developed. Predominantly theoretical types of mentality lack a mature self. Even Nietzsche, who attacks more passionately than anyone the judging conscience, derives the birth of the "inner man" from its appearance. In pointing to the subpersonal character of guilt and punishment in primitive cultures, he praises the discovery of the conscience as the elevation of mankind to a higher level. The fact that self and conscience are dependent on the experience of personal guilt explains the prevalence of the "bad conscience" in reality, literature, and theory. It supports the assertion that the uneasy, accusing, and judging conscience is the original phenomenon; that good conscience is only the absence of bad conscience; and that the demanding and warning conscience is only the anticipation of it. Since ego-self and conscience grow in mutual dependence, and since the self discovers itself in the experience of a split between what it is and what it ought to be, the basic character of the conscience—the conciousness of guilt—is obvious.

Shakespeare, in *King Richard III*, Act V, Scene 3, gives a classic expression of the relationship of individual self-consciousness, guilt, and conscience:

> Oh coward conscience, how dost thou afflict me! . . .
> What! do I fear myself? There's none else by.
> Richard loves Richard; that is, *I am I*.

> Is there a murderer here? No. Yes, I am.
> Then fly. What, from myself? Great reason why,
> Lest I revenge. What, *myself upon myself?*
> Alack, I love myself. Wherefore? For any good
> That I myself have done unto myself?
> O, no! alas, I rather hate myself. . . .
> My conscience hath a thousand several tongues,
> . . . crying all, Guilty! guilty.

In the next moment, however, Richard immerses himself in the we-consciousness of the battle, dismissing self and conscience:

> . . . conscience is a word that cowards use. . . .
> Our strong arms be our conscience, swords our law.
> March on, *join* bravely, let us to 't pell-mell;
> If not to heaven, then *hand in hand* to hell.

While the Old Testament describes the experience but not the notion of conscience (Adam, Cain, David, Job), the New Testament, especially Paul, has the word and the reality. Through the influence of Paul (who in this case, as in others, introduced elements of Hellenistic ethics into Christianity) conscience has become a common concept to the Christian nations, in their religious as well as secular periods.

Conscience, in the New Testament, has religious significance only indirectly. It has primarily an ethical meaning. The acceptance of the gospel, for instance, is not a demand of the conscience. It does not give laws, but it accuses and condemns him who has not fulfilled the law. Consequently, it is considered to be not a special quality of Christians but an element of human nature generally. In Romans 2:14—15, Paul expresses this very strongly: "When Gentiles who have no law obey instinctively the Law's requirements, they are a law to themselves, even though they have no law; they exhibit the effect of the Law written on their hearts, their conscience bears them witness, as their moral convictions accuse or, it may be, defend them" (Moffatt).

According to these words, the conscience witnesses to the law (either the Mosaic or the natural law), but it does not contain the law. Therefore its judgment can be wrong. Paul speaks of a "weak conscience" when describing the narrow and timid attitude of Christians who are afraid to buy meat in the market because it might have been used for sacrifices in pagan cults. Paul criticizes such attitudes. But he emphasizes that even an erring conscience must be obeyed, and he warns those who are strong in their conscience not to induce, by their example, those who are weak to do things that would give them an uneasy conscience. No higher estimation of the conscience as guide is possible. Paul does not say that we must follow it because it is right, but because disobedience to it means the loss of salvation (Romans 14). We can lose our salvation even when we do something objectively right, if we do it with an uneasy conscience. The unity and consistency of the moral personality are more important than its subjection to a truth that endangers this unity.

In principle, Christianity has always maintained the Pauline doctrine of conscience, the unconditional moral responsibility of the individual person. Aquinas and Luther agree on this point. Aquinas states that he must disobey the command of a superior to whom he has made a vow of obedience if the superior asks something against his conscience. And Luther's famous insistence, before the emperor in Worms, that it is not right to do something against the conscience (in this case to recant a theological insight) is based on the traditional Christian doctrine of conscience. But neither in Paul nor in Aquinas or Luther is the conscience a religious source. They all keep the authority of conscience within the ethical sphere. Luther's refusal to recant his doctrine of justification is an expression of his conscientiousness as a doctor of theology. He declares that he would recant if refuted by arguments taken from Scripture or reason, the positive source and the negative criterion of theology. But he does *not* say—as has been often stated by liberal Protestants—that his conscience is the *source* of his doctrine. There is no "religion of conscience" either in the New Testament or in classical Christianity before the sectarian movements of the Reformation period.

In the New Testament the relation of the moral conscience to faith as the foundation of the religious life is dealt with in only two connections. In Hebrews 9:9 ritual religion is criticized because "gifts and sacrifices . . . cannot possibly make the conscience of the worshiper perfect." Therefore, the writer continues, "Let us draw near with a true heart, in absolute assurance of faith, our hearts sprinkled clean from a bad conscience." Only perfect salvation can give the moral status from which a good conscience follows. But the "assurance of faith" is not a matter of conscience. The other link between faith and conscience is given in the criticism of heresy. Heresy entails an unclean conscience because it involves a moral distortion. In I Timothy 1:19 and 4:2 libertines and ascetics, both representatives of pagan dualistic morals, are rejected. Against them the writer says: "Hold to faith and a good conscience. Certain individuals have seared the good conscience and thus come to grief over their faith." They are "seared in conscience." The judgment that one cannot be a heretic with a good conscience has been accepted by the church. The moral implications of heresy were always emphasized, although not always rightly. Heresy is not an error in judgment or a difference in experience, but a demonic possession, splitting the moral self and producing a bad conscience. On this basis the church waged its war against the heretics of all periods.

Scholasticism raised the question: according to what norms does the conscience judge, and how are these norms recognized by it? The answer was given in terms of the artificial (or distorted) word *synteresis,* i.e., a perfection of our reason that leads us toward the recognition of the good. It has immediate and infallible evidence, being a spark of the divine light in us, the uncreated light in the depth of the soul, as the Franciscans asserted; the created light of our intuitive intellect, as the Dominicans said. The basic principles given by the *synteresis* are: (1) The good must be done; the evil must be avoided. (2) Every being must live according to nature. (3) Every being strives toward happiness. Conscience is the practical judgment that applies these principles to the concrete situation. It is *syllogismus practicus.* We are obliged to follow our conscience whether the *syllogismus* is correct or not. We are, of course, responsible for not knowing the good. But we are not allowed to act against our conscience, even if it is objectively correct to do so. Man has an infallible knowledge of the moral principles, the natural law, through *synteresis;* but he has a conscience that is able to fall into error in every concrete decision.

In order to prevent dangerous errors, the authorities of the church give advice to the Christian, especially in connection with the confession in the sacrament of penance. *Summae de casibus conscientiae* (collections concerning cases of conscience) were given to the priests. In this way the conscience became more and more dependent on the authority of the church. The immediate knowledge of the good was denied to the layman. The Jesuits removed the *synteresis,* and with it any direct contact between God and man, replacing it by the ecclesiastical, and especially the Jesuit, adviser. But the adviser had the choice from among different authorities, since the opinion of each of them was equally probable. Heteronomy and probabilism destroyed the autonomous, self-assured conscience.

In spite of these distortions, the medieval development

performed a tremendous task in educating and refining the conscience of the European people generally, and the monastic and semimonastic groups in particular. The depth and breadth of bad conscience in the later Middle Ages is the result of this education and the soil for new interpretations of the meaning and functions of conscience.

Turning to the "sectarian" understanding of conscience, we find the Franciscan idea of the immediate knowledge of the natural law in the depth of the human soul. But two new elements supported and transformed this tradition: the so-called "German mysticism," with its emphasis on the divine spark in the human soul, and the "spiritual enthusiasm" awakened by the Reformation, with its emphasis on the individual possession of the Spirit. Thomas Muenzer and all his sectarian followers taught that the divine Spirit speaks to us out of the depth of our own soul. *We* are not speaking to ourselves, but God within us. "Out of the abyss of the heart which is from the living God," wrote Muenzer, we receive the truth if we are opened to it by suffering. Since the enthusiasts understood this divine voice within us in a very concrete sense, they identified it with the conscience. In this way conscience became a source of religious insight and not simply a judge of moral actions. The conscience as the expression of the inward light has a revealing character.

But the question arose immediately: what is the content of such a revelation through conscience? Luther asked Muenzer, and Cromwell asked Fox: what is the difference between practical reason and the inward light? Both of them could answer: the ecstatic character of the divine Spirit! But they could be asked again: what bearing has the ecstatic form of revelation on its content? And then the answer was difficult. Muenzer referred to practical decisions in his daily life, made under the inspiration of the Spirit; and Fox developed an ethics of unconditional honesty, bourgeois righteousness, and pacifism. It was easy to ask again whether reasonableness and obedience to the natural moral law could not produce the same results. The "revealing conscience" is a union of mysticism with moral rationality. But it does not reveal anything beyond biblical and genuine Christian tradition.

An important result arising from this transformation of the concept of conscience is the idea of tolerance and its victory in the liberal era. The quest for "freedom of conscience" does not refer to the concrete ethical decision, but to the religious authority of the inward light that expresses itself through the individual conscience. And since the inward light could hardly be distinguished from practical reason, freedom of conscience meant, actually, the freedom to follow one's autonomous reason, not only in ethics, but also in religion. The "religion of conscience" and the consequent idea of tolerance are not a result of the Reformation, but of sectarian spiritualism and mysticism.

The modern philosophical interpretation of conscience follows three main lines: an emotional-aesthetic line, an abstract-formalistic line, and a rational-idealistic line. Secularizing the sectarian belief in the revealing power of conscience, Shaftesbury interprets it as the emotional reaction to the harmony between self-relatedness and relatedness to others, in all beings and in the universe as a whole. The principle of ethical action is the balance between the effects of benevolence and the effects of selfishness as indicated by conscience. Conscience works better and more accurately, the more the taste for the universe and its harmony is developed. The educated conscience has a perfect ethical taste. Not harmony with the universe but sympathy with the other man is the basis of conscience, according to Hume and Adam Smith; we identify ourselves with the other man and take his approval or disapproval of our action as our own judgment. This, of course, presupposes a hidden harmony between individuals and the possibility of a mutual feeling of identification. It presupposes a universal principle of harmony in which individuals participate and which reveals itself to the conscience.

The emotional-harmonistic interpretation of conscience has often led to a replacement of ethical by aesthetic principles. The attitude of late aristocracy, high *bourgeoisie,* and bohemianism at the end of the last century was characterized by the elevation of good taste to be the ultimate judge in moral affairs, corresponding to the replacement of religion by the arts in these groups. It was an attempt to reach a transmoral conscience but it did not reach even a moral one, and it was swept away by the revolutionary morality and immorality of the twentieth century.

The second method of interpreting conscience philosophically is the abstract-formalistic one. It was most clearly stated by Kant, and it was introduced into theology by Ritschl. Kant wanted to maintain the unconditional character of the moral demand against all emotional relativism, against fear and pleasure motives, as well as against divine and human authorities. But in doing so he was driven to a complete formalism. Conscience is the consciousness of the "categorical [unconditional] imperative," but it is not the consciousness of a special content of this imperative. "Conscience is a consciousness which itself is a duty." It is a duty to have a conscience, to be conscientious. The content, according to Ritschl, is dependent on the special vocation, a special historical time and space. Only conscientiousness is always demanded. This corresponds to the Protestant, especially the Lutheran, evaluation of work. It is the expression of the activistic element of the *bourgeoisie* and is identical with the bourgeois adaptation to the technical and psychological demands of the economic system. Duty is what serves bourgeois production. This is the hidden meaning even of the philosophy of the "absolute ego" in Fichte, who describes conscience as the certainty of the pure duty that is independent of anything besides its transcendent freedom. In the moment when transcendent freedom comes down to action it is transformed into obedience to a well-calculated system of economic services. It is understandable that this loss of a concrete direction of conscientiousness paved the way for immoral contents when they were commanded, for instance, by a totalitarian state.

Against the aesthetic-emotional as well as the authoritarian form of determining the conscience, attempts were made in modern philosophy to have rationality and contents united. The most influential of these attempts is the common-sense theory of Thomas Reid and the Scottish school, i.e., the moral sense is common to everybody, being a natural endowment of human nature (like the *synteresis* of the scholastics). Decisive for practical ethics is Hutcheson's theory of the sense of benevolence toward others. This theory adequately expresses the reality of British (and to a degree, American) conformism and natural benevolence in a society where the converging tendencies still prevail over the diverging ones, and in which a secularized Christian morality is still dominant.

Another attempt to find rational contents for the conscience was made by Hegel. He distinguishes the formal and the true conscience. About the first he says, "Conscience is the infinite formal certainty of oneself—it expresses the absolute right of the subjective self-consciousness—namely, to know within and out of itself what law and duty are, and to acknowledge nothing except what it knows in this way as the good." But this subjectivity is fallible and may turn into error and guilt. Therefore, it needs content in order to become the true conscience. This content is the reality of family, society, and state. With the state (as the organization of historical reason) the formal conscience is transformed into the true conscience. It is a mistake to link these ideas historically to the totalitarian use of the state and the pagan distortion of conscience by national socialism. Hegel was a rationalist, not a positivist. His idea of the state unites Christian-conservative and bourgeois-liberal elements. His famous, though rarely understood, idea of the state as the "god on earth" is based on the identification of the state with the church as the "body of Christ," expressed in secular terms. The conscience that is determined by the state in this sense is determined not by bureaucratic orders but by the life of a half-religious, half-secular organism—the counterpart of the Christian-rationalistic common sense of the Anglo-Saxon society.

While the Scottish solution is largely dependent on the social attitude of Western Christianity and Hegel's solution on Lutheran Protestantism, the spirit of Catholicism has received a new philosophical expression in recent philosophical developments, of which I take Max Scheler as a representative. In his doctrine of conscience, Scheler opposes the popular conception of conscience as the "voice of God." He calls this, as well as the quest for "freedom of conscience," a principle of chaos. Instead of freedom of conscience, he demands subjection to authority as the only way of experiencing the intuitive evidence for moral principles. It is impossible to reach such evidence without personal experience, and it is impossible to have such an experience without acting under the guidance of an authority that is based on former experience. In this respect, ethical (we could say "existential") experience is different from theoretical (i.e., "detached") experience. Although this completely fits the situation of the Catholic, it is not meant as the establishment of external authority. "All authority is concerned only with the good which is universally evident, never with that which is individually evident." Ethical authority is based on general ethical evidence. But does such a general ethical evidence exist? Or is philosophical ethics bound to be either general and abstract or to be concrete and dependent on changing historical conditions? And if this is the alternative, can the problem of conscience be answered at all in terms of *moral* conscience?

A conscience may be called "transmoral" if it judges not in obedience to a moral law, but according to its participation in a reality that transcends the sphere of moral commands. A transmoral conscience does not deny the moral realm, but is driven beyond it by the unbearable tensions of the sphere of law.

It was Luther who derived a new concept of conscience from the experience of justification through faith; neither Paul nor Augustine did so. Luther's experience grew out of the monastic scrutiny of conscience and the threat of the ultimate judgment, which he felt in its full depth and horror. Experiences like these he called *Anfechtungen*, that is, "tempting attacks," stemming from Satan as the tool of the divine wrath. These attacks are the most terrible thing a human being can experience. They create an incredible *Angst* ("dread"), a feeling of being enclosed in a narrow place from which there is no escape. (*Angst*, he rightly pointed out, is derived from *angustiae*, "narrows.") "Thou drivest me from the surface of the earth," he cries to God in despair, even in hate. Luther describes this situation in many different ways. He compares the horrified conscience that tries to flee and cannot escape, with a goose that, pursued by the wolf, does not use its wings, as ordinarily, but its feet, and is caught. Or he tells us how the moving of dry leaves frightens him as the expression of the wrath of God. His conscience confirms the divine wrath and judgment. God says to him, "Thou canst not judge differently about thyself." Such experiences are not dependent on special sins. The self, as such, is sinful before any act; it is separated from God, unwilling to love Him.

If in this way bad conscience is deepened into a state of absolute despair, it can be conquered only by the acceptance of God's self-sacrificing love as visible in the picture of Jesus as the Christ. God, so to speak, subjects Himself to the consequences of His wrath, taking them upon Himself, thus reestablishing unity with us. The sinner is accepted as just in spite of his sinfulness. The wrath of God does not frighten us any longer; a joyful conscience arises as much *above* the moral realm as the desperate conscience was *below* the moral realm. "Justification by grace," in Luther's sense, means the creation of a "transmoral" conscience. While God is the accuser in the *Anfechtung* and our heart tries to excuse itself, in the "justification" our heart accuses us and God defends us against ourselves. In psychological terms this means: insofar as we look at ourselves, we must experience a desperate conscience; insofar as we look at the power of a new creation beyond ourselves, we can attain a joyful conscience. Not because of our moral perfection, but in spite of our moral imperfection, we are fighting and triumphing on the side of God. As in Dürer's famous painting, "Knight, Death, and the Devil," the knight goes through the narrows in the attitude of victorious defiance of dread and temptation.

An analogy to this "triumphant conscience," as developed by Luther personally as well as theologically, appeared in the enthusiastic philosophy of Giordano Bruno. The moral conscience is overcome by the "heroic affect" toward the universe and the surrender to its infinity and inexhaustible creativity. Participation in the creativity of life universal liberates the moral conscience, the bad as well as the good. Man, standing in the center of being, is bound to transform life as it is into higher life. He takes upon himself the tragic consequences, connected with the destructive side of finite creativity, and must not try to escape them for the sake of a good moral conscience.

While in Bruno the transmoral conscience is based on a mystical naturalism, Nietzsche's transmoralism is a consequence of his dramatic-tragic naturalism. Nietzsche belongs to those empiricists who have tried to analyze the genesis of moral conscience in such a way that its autonomy is destroyed—Hobbes and Helvetius, on the ground of a materialistic metaphysics; Mandeville and Bentham, on the ground of a utilitarian psychology; Darwin and Freud, on the ground of an evolutionary naturalism—all have denied any objective validity to the voice of conscience, according to their rejection of any universal natural (rational) law. Nietzsche carried these ideas further, as the title and the content of *Genealogy of Morals* show. He says, "The bad conscience is a sickness, but it is a sickness as pregnancy is one." It is a creative sickness. Mankind had to be domesticated, and this has been done by its conquerors and ruling classes. It was in the interest of these classes to suppress by severe punishments the natural instincts of aggressiveness, will to power, destruction, cruelty, revolution. They succeeded in suppressing these trends. But they did not succeed in eradicating them. So the aggressive instincts became internalized and transformed into self-destructive tendencies. Man has turned against himself in self-punishment; he is separated from his animal past from which he had derived strength, joy, and creativity. But he cannot prevent his instincts from remaining alive. They require permanent acts of suppression, the result of which is the bad conscience, a great thing in man's evolution, an ugly thing if compared with man's real aim.

Nietzsche describes this aim in terms which remind one of Luther's descriptions of the transmoral conscience: "Once in a stronger period than our morbid, desperate present, he must appear, the man of the great love and the great contempt, the creative spirit who does now allow his driving strength to be turned to a transcendent world." Nietzsche calls him the man "who is strong through wars and victories, who needs conquest, adventure, danger, even pain." This man is "beyond good and evil" in the moral sense. At the same time, he is

good in the metaphysical (or mystical) sense that he is in unity
with life universal. He has a transmoral conscience, not on
the basis of a paradoxical unity with God (such as Luther
has), but on the basis of an enthusiastic unity with life in its
creative and destructive power.

Recent "existential" philosophy has developed a doctrine
of transmoral conscience that follows the general lines of
Luther, Bruno, and Nietzsche. Heidegger, the main representative of existential philosophy, says, "The call of conscience has the character of the demand that man in his finitude
actualize his genuine potentialities, and this means an appeal
to become guilty." Conscience summons us to ourselves,
calling us back from the talk of the market and the conventional behavior of the masses. It has no special demands; it
speaks to us in the "mode of silence." It tells us only to act
and to become guilty by acting, for every action is unscrupu-
lous. He who acts experiences the call of conscience and, at
the same time, has the experience of contradicting his conscience, of being guilty. "Existence as such is guilty." Only
self-deception can give a good moral conscience, since it is
impossible *not* to act and since every action implies guilt. We
must act, and the attitude in which we *can* act is "resoluteness."
Resoluteness transcends the moral conscience, its arguments
and prohibitions. It determines a situation instead of being
determined by it. *The good, transmoral conscience consists in
the acceptance of the bad, moral conscience,* which is unavoidable whenever decisions are made and acts are performed.

The way from Luther's to Heidegger's idea of a transmoral
conscience was a dangerous one. "Transmoral" can mean the
re-establishment of morality from a point above morality, or
it can mean the destruction of morality from a point below
morality. The empiricists from Hobbes to Freud have analyzed
moral conscience, but they have not destroyed it. Either they
were dependent in their concrete ethics on Anglo-Saxon

common sense; or they identified utility with the social conventions of a well-established *bourgeoisie;* or they cultivated a high sense of conscientiousnes, in scientific honesty as well as in the fulfillment of duties; or they did not dare, unconsciously or consciously, to draw the radical moral consequences of their dissolution of the conscience. In Nietzsche and Heidegger none of these inhibitions is left. But it is not without *some* justification that these names are connected with the antimoral movements of fascism or national socialism. Even Luther has been linked with them, as have Machiavelli and Bruno.

This raises the questions: is the idea of a transmoral conscience tenable? Or is it so dangerous that it cannot be maintained? But if the idea must be dismissed, religion as well as analytic psychotherapy would also have to be dismissed. For in both of them, the moral conscience is transcendent—in religion by the acceptance of the divine grace that breaks through the realm of law and creates a joyful conscience, and in depth psychology by the acceptance of one's own conflicts when looking at them and suffering under their ugliness without an attempt to suppress them and to hide them from oneself. Indeed, it is impossible *not* to transcend the moral conscience because it is impossible to unite a *sensitive* and a *good* conscience. Those who have a sensitive conscience cannot escape the question of the transmoral conscience. The moral conscience drives beyond the sphere in which it is valid to the sphere from which it must receive its conditional validity.

V

Ethics in a
Changing World

"Changing World" in the title of this chapter does not mean
the general change implied in everything that exists. Neither
does it mean the continuous change involved more fundamentally with history than with nature. But it points to the fact that
we are living in a historical period, characterized by a radical
and revolutionary transformation of one historical era into
another. Nobody can doubt this fact seriously, and nobody
who has even a minimum of historical understanding would
do so after what has occurred during recent years. We are in
the midst of a world revolution affecting every section of
human existence, forcing upon us a new interpretation of
life and the world.

What about ethics in this connection? Does it represent a
realm above change? Is it suprahistorical in its foundation,
its values, and its commands? Or does it follow the stream of
historical becoming, and will it be transformed as rapidly as the
other realms of life are transformed in our days? If the latter
be true, what authority, what power of shaping human life
remains in it? Can the unconditional claim with which every
moral demand imposes itself on human conscience be maintained if the contents of the demand are different in every
period of history? But if the former be the case—if ethics
constitutes a realm above history, immovable and uncon-

cerned by historical change—how can it influence man, living in history and transformed by history? Would it not remain a strange body within the context of human experience, separated from it in untouchable remoteness, perhaps worthy of awe but without actual influence on the life-process?

In order to answer these questions and to make them pertinent to our present situation, I intend to deal, first, with some solutions that have already appeared in the history of human thought, and are still of great actual importance; second, I wish to give my own solution; and, third, I will try to apply this solution to the present world-situation by giving some practical examples.

There are three great types of life and thought representing three different solutions of the problem of ethics in historical change: first, the static supranaturalistic solution, represented by the Roman Catholic church and expressed in the ethics of Thomas Aquinas; second, the dynamic-naturalistic solution, represented by the National Socialist movement and expressed in the ethics of the philosophers of life; third, the rationalistic-progressive solution, represented by Anglo-Saxon common sense and expressed in the ethics of the philosophers of reason.

With tremendous psychological power the static supranaturalistic solution maintains the eternal and immovable character of the ethical norms and commands. Philosophy and theology co-operate in this direction. The world is conceived as a system of eternal structures, preformed in the divine mind, which are substance and essence of everything and which establish the norms and laws for man's personal and social practice. Philosophy discovers these structures and laws, and revelation confirms and amends them. Revelation adds some superstructures of its own that are new and higher laws, but equally eternal and immovable. Both the natural and the supranatural structures together form a hierarchy of powers and values that control nature and are supposed to control human activities. The church, itself a hierarchical system, teaches this system, educates for it, fights for its political realization, and defends it against new systems. But in so doing the church cannot disregard the actual situation and historical changes. The church must adapt its ethical system to new problems and new demands. The Catholic church has been able to do just this, admirably, for centuries, and the living authority of the Pope is still a marvelous instrument for achieving adaptations without losing its immovable basis.

Nevertheless, it is obvious that the Catholic church did not fully succeed in dealing with the presuppositions and demands of the bourgeois era. Protestantism and the Enlightenment created new systems of ethics standing in opposition to the supposedly eternal system of the medieval church. And when the church tried to proceed with the stream of the rising *bourgeoisie,* as, for example, in the moral preachings of seventeenth- and eighteenth-century Jesuitism and in the teachings of nineteenth-century modernism, either it lost its seriousness and authority or it gave the unhappy impression of rearguard action in which every position is defended as long as possible and then surrendered. And the important utterances of the Holy See during the nineteenth century concerning social and political problems presuppose, in order to be applicable, the unbroken unity and authority of the Christian church, which no longer exist. Therefore, they did not at all influence the spirit of modern ethics and the direction of bourgeois society. The price paid by the static supranaturalistic answer to our question has been the loss of a determining influence on the changing world of the last centuries.

The opposite solution, represented by national socialism, was prepared for in two main ways—by the Continental vitalistic philosophy and by Anglo-American positivism and pragmatism, the latter being only a different form of the vitalistic philosophy. National Socialism has used and abused the philosophical motives of the Continental philosophy of life, especially of Nietzsche, Pareto, and Sorel. Philosophy must express life in its changing forms and trends. Truth, according to Nietzsche, is that lie which is useful for particular species of being. Values are produced and withdrawn in the dynamic process of life—biologically speaking, by the strongest kind of living beings; sociologically speaking, by the new élite; and politically speaking, by the eruptive violence of a revolutionary group. Change, being the chief character of life, is also the chief character of ethics. There are no independent norms above life, no criteria by which power can be judged, no standards for a good life. Good life is strong life, or violent life, or the life of a ruling aristocracy, or the life of conquering race. This implies that the individual, instead of being guided by the ethical norms that are manifest in his conscience, is obliged to merge his conscience with the group conscience. He must co-ordinate his standards with the group standards, as represented by the leaders of the group. The dynamic-naturalistic type of answer to the question of ethics in a changing world has a primitive-tribal character. It is, historically speaking, at the same time the most recent and the most ancient of all solutions of the ethical problem.

I have mentioned Anglo-Saxon positivism and pragmatism in this connection. It is an important task of this chapter to make it clear that pragmatism and vitalistic philosophy belong to the same type of ethical dynamism. When pragmatism speaks of experience, it surrenders the criteria of truth and the good no less than does vitalistic philosophy. There are for it no norms above the dynamic process of experience, that is, of experienced life. The question of what kind of life creates ethical experience and what the standards of a true ethical experience are is not answered and cannot be answered within the context of pragmatic thought. Therefore, the pragmatists and the positivists take their refuge in an ethical instinct, that is supposed to lead to an ethical common sense. This refuge is secure so long as there is a society with a strong common belief and conventional morals maintained by the leading groups of society. Such was the situation in the acme of the bourgeois development, for instance, in the Victorian era. But it was no longer effective when the harmony of a satisfied society slowly dissolved, and dissatisfied groups, masses, and nations asked for a new order of life. The ethical instinct of those groups was very different from the ethical instincts of the ascendant Victorian *bourgeoisie,* and the refuge in ethical instinct and common sense became ineffective. Pragmatism and positivism were unable to face this threat, because, in their basic ideas, they agree with the principles of the philosophy of life.

The intellectual defense of Anglo-Saxon civilization against fascist ideologies is extremely weak. Common-sense philosophy and pragmatism are not able to provide criteria against the dynamic irrationalism of the new movements; and they are not able to awaken the moral power of resistance necessary for the maintenance of the humanistic values embodied in Western and Anglo-Saxon civilization. It is not positivism and pragmatism, but the remnants of the rationalistic-progressive solution of the ethical problem on which the future of that civilization is based. The solution is the most natural one for undisturbed bourgeois thought and is still deeply rooted in the subconscious of contemporary philosophers as well as of laymen.

There are, according to this point of view, some eternal principles, the natural law of morals, but without the supranatural sanction claimed for it in the Catholic system. These principles, as embodied in the Bill of Rights, are like stars that always remain remote from every human realization but that, like stars, show the direction in which mankind must go. Once discovered, they cannot disappear again, although their theoretical and practical realization is always in process toward a higher perfection. In this way they are adaptable to every human situation.

Is this the solution of the problem of ethics in a changing world? In some ways it is, in some ways not. It indicates the direction in which the solution must be sought. There must be something immovable in the ethical principle, the criterion and standard of all ethical change. There must be a power of change within the ethical principle itself. And both must be united. But the rationalistic-progressive solution is far from reaching this unity. It establishes some principles, such as freedom and equality, in the name of the absolute natural law to be found in nature and human reason at any time and in any place. Mankind is supposed to realize these principles, theoretically and practically, in a process of approximation. It is the same natural law, the same principles that always have been more or less known, more or less received in reality. "More or less" points to a quantitative difference, not to a qualitative change, not to new creations in the ethical realm. Ethics in a changing world changes only quantitatively, that is, as far as progress or regression with respect to their realization is concerned. More or less freedom and more or less equality are admitted, but not a new freedom or a new equality.

But the principles on which the progressive-rationalistic solution is based represent a special pattern, a special type of freedom and equality, that of the later ancient and that of the modern bourgeois period. They do not represent principles comprehensive enough to embrace all periods and creative enough to bring new embodiments of themselves. They are not eternal enough to be ultimate principles and not temporal enough to fit a changing world. Therefore, as the Catholic system was not able to adapt itself seriously to the modern period of bourgeois growth, so the bourgeois-progressive rationalism was not able to face the breakdown of the bourgeois world. Supranatural and rational absolutism in ethics both proved to be unable to adapt themselves to a fundamental change in the historical situation.

Is there a possible solution beyond the alternative of an absolutism that breaks down in every radical change of history and a relativism that makes change itself the ultimate principle? I believe that there is, and I think it is implied in the basis of Christian ethics, namely, in the principle of love in the sense of the Greek word *agape*. This is not said in terms of an apology for Christianity, but under the impetus of the actual problem in our present world-situation. Love, *agape*, offers a principle of ethics that maintains an eternal, unchangeable element, but makes its realization dependent on continuous acts of a creative intuition. Love is above law, and also above the natural law in Stoicism and the supranatural law in Catholicism. We *can* express it as a law; we can say as Jesus and the apostles did, "Thou shalt love." But in doing so, we know that this is a paradoxical way of speaking, indicating that the ultimate principle of ethics, which, on the one hand, is an unconditional command, is, on the other hand, the power breaking through all commands. And just this ambiguous character of love enables it to be the solution of the question of ethics in a changing world.

If we look at the principles of natural law as embodied in the Bill of Rights, we will discover that, taken as the concrete embodiments of the principle of love in a special situation, they are great and true and powerful; they represent love by establishing freedom and equal rights against willfulness and suppression and the destruction of the dignity of human beings. But, taken as eternal laws and applied legalistically to different situations—for example, the early Middle Ages, or the decay and transformation of economic capitalism—these principles become bad ideologies used for the maintenance of decaying institutions and powers. This is why Paul and Luther struggled so profoundly against the "Law," and why they insisted on the deadening consequences of the law and the vivifying power of love. *Love alone can transform itself according to the concrete demands of every individual and social situation without losing its eternity and dignity and unconditional validity.* Love can adapt itself to every phase of a changing world.

I should like to introduce at this point another Greek word, *kairos,* "the right time." This word, used in everyday Greek, received an emphatic meaning in the language of the New Testament, designating the fulfillment of time in the appearance of the Christ. It has been reinterpreted by German religious socialism in the sense of a special gift and a special task, breaking from eternity into history at a special time. *Kairos* in this sense is the historical moment when something new, eternally important, manifests itself in temporal forms, in the potentialities and tasks of a special period. It is the power of the prophetic spirit in all periods of history to pronounce the coming of such a *kairos,* to discover its meaning, and to express the criticism of what is given and the hope for what is to come.

All great changes in history are accompanied by a strong consciousness of a *kairos* at hand. Therefore, ethics in a changing world must be understood as ethics of the *kairos.* The answer to the demand for ethics in a changing world is ethics determined by the *kairos.* But only love is able to appear in every *kairos.* Law is not able, because law is the attempt to impose what belonged to a special time on all times. An ideal that appeared at the right time and was valid for this time is now considered to be the ideal for history as a whole, as that form of life in which history shall find its end. The outcome of this attitude is inevitably disillusionment and the rise of ethical libertarianism and relativism. This is the point at which the dynamic-naturalistic solution, despite its destructive consequences, was in the right, and still battles rightly against Catholic and bourgeois ethics. Or, expressed in terms of church history, this is the point at which Luther was right in his opposition to Aquinas and Calvin. Love, realizing itself from *kairos* to *kairos*, creates an ethics that is beyond the alternatives of absolute and relative ethics.

This solution can be clarified by some concrete examples. Let us consider the idea of equality, one of the foundations of rationalistic-progressive ethics. In the light of the principle of love, and in the perspective of the idea of *kairos*, the following can be said: love implies equality in some respect. He who loves and he who is loved are equal to each other insofar as they are worthy of love, the one for the other. However, nothing but precisely this principle of equality is implied—*essentially* implied—in love. Everything else is a historical embodiment of that principle in different situations, with love and the distortion of love at the same time. Looking at a Greek city-state, we discover that there is a political equality among individuals in a special group, and to a certain extent among all those who are free; but there is an absolute inequality between the free and the slave. Love is not manifest as *the* principle; but since it is potentially the principle, it is effective even in the religion and culture of Apollo and Dionysus. It is effective in the kind of equality that the city-state gives to those who belong to it, excluding slaves and barbarians. Love is effective even in this restricted equality, but it is a restricted, distorted love—love within the boundaries of national pride and racial discrimination. The central *kairos* in which love becomes manifest as what it really is has not yet appeared.

Nor did it appear in the period of the universal Roman empire, when Stoicism extended equality to all human beings

— men and women, children and slaves. Here the principle of love broke through the limitations of national and social arrogance, but it did so as a universal, rational law, and not as love. Stoic equality is universal, but cool and abstract, without the warmth and the communal element of the limited equality in the city-state. At its best, it is participation in Roman citizenship and implies the possibility of a man's becoming wise. In the Christian message, love becomes manifest in its universality, and, at the same time, in its concreteness: the "neighbor" is the immediate object of love, and everyone can become "neighbor." All inequalities between men are overcome insofar as men are potential children of God. But this did not lead Christianity to the Stoic idea of equality. Not even the inequality between lord and slave was attacked, except in the realm of the Christian community. Later, not the totalitarian but the hierarchical principle was supported by the Christian church in accord with late ancient and medieval society. The social and psychological inequalities of the feudal order did not seem to contradict the element of equality implied in the principle of love. On the contrary, the mutual interpendence of all the degrees of the hierarchy, the solidarity of all the members of a medieval city, and the patriarchalistic care of the feudal lords for the "people," were considered the highest form of equality demanded by the principle of love.

In bourgeois liberalism, equality was again interpreted in terms of the general natural law, the law of reason and humanity. Equality became equality before the law and the demand for equal economic opportunities. This was in accord with the principle of love over against the tyranny and injustice into which the older system had developed. But in the measure by which the equal opportunity of everybody became a mere ideology to cover the exclusive opportunity of a few, the liberal idea of equality became a contradiction of love. A new idea of equality arose, conceiving the equal security of everyone, even at the sacrifice of much political equality. One must not condemn the collectivistic and authoritarian forms of equality just because they negate equality's liberal and democratic forms. Love may demand a transformation in this *kairos*. A new creative realization of the element of equality as implied in the principle of love may be brought about in our period. It will be good insofar as it is in better accord with the demands of love in our special situation than were the feudal and liberal forms. It will be bad insofar as it will become a distortion and contradiction of love. For love is eternal, although it creates something new in each *kairos*.

I could refer to many other ethical problems in order to demonstrate their double dependence on the principle of love, on the one hand, and on the changing *kairos*, on the other. For example, I could point to the evaluation of work and activism in the different periods of history and their relation to leisure and meditation. It is obvious that a coming collectivism will reduce the emphasis on work and activism considerably by restraining the principle of competition. As the struggle against some forms of feudal and ecclesiastical leisure and meditative life was a demand for love in the period of the decaying Middle Ages, and occurred at the time when mankind began to control nature, so it is now a demand of love and *kairos* that leisure and meditation return in terms of a new more collectivistic structure of society over against a self-destructive adoration of work and activism.

Other examples are the problems of asceticism and wordliness, of self-control and self-expression, of discipline and creativity, in their relation to each other. Both sides of these contrasts follow from the principle of love. The negation of the first aspect would prevent the self-surrender implied in love; the negation of the second would destroy any subject worthy of love. It depends on the *kairos* as to which of these aspects, in which form and in which balance with the other, is emphasized. For our present stage, neither the supranatural asceticism of the Catholic system nor the rational self-control of bourgeois society, nor the naturalistic war-and-state discipline of fascism can provide the solution. And the same is true of feudal eroticism, of bourgeois aestheticism, and of the fascist idolatry of vitality. Another solution is demanded by love and by *kairos*.

Psychoanalysis provides some elements of the solution, although mere psychotherapeutic psychology is not able to create by itself a new system of ethics. Other elements of the solution are suggested by the rediscovery of the classical meaning of *eros*, and by the different attempts to relate it to *agape*. Educational movements and criticism of the bourgeois ideal of the family have contributed a great deal. But everything is in motion, and the criterion of the final solution is the measure by which *eros*, on the one hand, and self-control, on the other, are shaped by love.

A final question must be answered. If love is the principle of ethics, and if *kairos* is the manner of its embodiment in concrete contents, how can a permanent uncertainty, a continous criticism which destroys the seriousness of the ethical demand, be avoided? Is not law and are not institutions necessary in order to maintain the actual ethical process? Indeed, law and institutions are required. They are required by love itself. For every individual, even the most creative, needs given structures that embody the experience and wisdom of the past, that liberate him from the necessity of having to make innumerable decisions on his own, and that show him a meaningful way to act in most situations. On this point Catholicism was superior in love both to Protestantism and to liberalism. And this is the reason why the younger generation in many countries eagerly demands laws and institutions to relieve them of their unbearable burden of having to make continuous ultimate decisions. No system of ethics can ever become an actual power without laws and institutions. Luther, in his great emphasis on the creativity of love, forgot this necessity. This is one of the reasons why the moral education of the masses in Germany is less thorough than in the Calvinistic countries. On the other hand, there is a greater readiness for a *kairos* in Germany than there is in the more thoroughly educated and normalized Western nations. Love demands laws and institutions, but love is always able to break through them in a new *kairos,* and to create new laws and new systems of ethics.

I have not mentioned the word "justice" in this chapter. It would be misleading in the present discussion because it is generally understood in the sense of the abstract natural law of Stoicism and rationalism. As such, it is either empty or is the concrete law of a special period, and is thus without universal validity. If justice is taken concretely, it means the laws and institutions in which love is embodied in a special situation. The Platonic ideal of justice was the concrete harmony of the city-state. In Israel, justice was the pious obedience to the commands of God. In medieval feudalism, it was the form of mutual responsibility of all levels of the hierarchy to each other. The liberal idea of justice was the abolition of formal privileges and the introduction of legal equality. In the more collectivistic society of the future, justice will be the system of laws and forms by which a sufficient security of the whole, and of all members, will be developed and maintained. It follows, then, that justice is the secondary and derived principle, while love, actualized from *kairos* to *kairos,* is the creative and basic principle.

I have given no definition of love. This is impossible because there is no higher principle by which it can be defined.

It is life itself in its actual unity. The forms and structures in which love embodies itself are the forms and structures in which life is possible, in which life overcomes its self-destructive forces. And this is the meaning of ethics: the expression of the ways in which love embodies itself, and life is maintained and saved.

Printed in the United States
200105BV00008B/151-225/A